Double·Take
Sewing™

Text by Carol Zentgraf

Edited by Jeanne Stauffer

HOUSE of
WHITE
BIRCHES
PUBLISHERS
SINCE 1947

Double-Take Sewing

Copyright © 2003 House of White Birches, Berne, Indiana 46711

Editor: Jeanne Stauffer
Associate Editors: Dianne Schmidt, Barb Sprunger
Contributing Editor: Vicki Blizzard
Technical Editor: Mary Jo Kurten
Book and Cover Design: Jessi Butler, Ronda Bechinski
Copy Editors: Michelle Beck, Mary Martin, Nicki Lehman

Photography: Jeff Chilcote, Tammy Christian, Kelly Heydinger, Nancy Sharp, Justin Wiard
Photography Assistant: Linda Quinlan

Graphic Artist: Ronda Bechinski
Production Assistants: Janet Bowers, Marj Morgan
Technical Artists: Liz Morgan, Travis Spangler, Chad Summers
Traffic Coordinator: Sandra Beres

Publishers: Carl H. Muselman, Arthur K. Muselman
Chief Executive Officer: John Robinson
Publishing Marketing Director: David McKee
Book Marketing Manager: Craig Scott
Product Development Director: Vivian Rothe
Publishing Services Director: Brenda R. Wendling
Publishing Services Manager: Brenda Gallmeyer

Printed in the United States of America
First Printing: 2003
Library of Congress Number: 2001097997
ISBN: 1-882138-95-3

Welcome!

Discover the versatility of sewing projects with looks that can be transformed in an instant! Using the tips and techniques featured in this book, you can create two different projects in little more time than it takes to make one.

Consider the possibilities—vests and jackets that change with the seasons or transform from casual to dressy in the time it takes to turn them inside out. Reversible table treatments and accent pillows can change the ambiance of a room in an instant.

Think of the time you'll save when you create multiholiday accents for your home— a trick-or-treat basket that serves double duty a month later as a scented pinecone holder. You'll never again want to sew a project that doesn't reverse.

Warm regards,

Jeanne Stauffer

Contents

Introduction

By Carol Zentgraf

Do you believe in magic? You will, once you enter the wonderful world of reversible sewing. Not only will you discover the versatility of projects with looks that transform in an instant, but you'll also be thrilled at their time- and money-saving attributes.

Using the techniques featured throughout this book, you can essentially create two different projects in the same time it takes to sew one project. You'll also save money on fabric, thread and trims, as well as other accents, such as closures.

And best of all, the possibilities are endless. Whether you're creating garments, accessories or home décor accents, your choice of looks is limited only by your imagination.

Consider the possiblities—jackets, vests and skirts that change with the seasons or transform from casual to dressy as easily as turning them inside out, or hats, scarves, belts and handbags that can each enhance an ensemble with a choice of two looks. Contrasting collars and cuffs that turn back are naturally easy to create when sewing a reversible garment, as are beautiful "lined effects" on hats and handbags. You'll find within the following chapters projects that are the perfect way to expand your wardrobe, and also make wonderful gifts.

Reversible sewing for the home is equally wonderful. In an instant you can change a room's ambiance by reversing window treatments, duvet covers, table treatments or accent pillows. How about a quick way to cover a utility shelf for children's toys that will grow up with them as their tastes change from *Sesame Street* to baseball or fairy princesses? Our clever storage unit cover offers two totally different looks: one touched with whimsy for a tot's delight, while the other showcases the tastes of an older child. Think of how much time you can save once the busy fall months arrive when you create multiseasonal accents for your home. A trick-or-treat basket covered with a fun-loving fall print serves double duty a month later as a scented pinecone holder covered with Christmas fabric.

Using the techniques featured throughout this book, you can essentially create two different projects in the same time it takes to sew one project.

What makes a project reversible? The answers lie in the pages to follow. Proper fabric and pattern selections ensure your sewing pleasure and the project's success. Special seam and edge finishes, turning techniques and closure applications give your projects the professional results you desire. It's all waiting for you, so gather some favorite fabrics and trims and get started. You may never want to sew a project that doesn't reverse again. ✄

Getting Started!

The first steps in creating a reversible project are choosing a pattern and fabric. Many of the featured accessories and home décor projects don't require a purchased pattern, and those that do need no or minimal pattern adjustments.

The key to success is selecting an appropriate pattern, making pattern adjustments and selecting compatible fabrics.

Sewing a reversible garment from a purchased pattern calls for more considerations. The key to success is selecting an appropriate pattern, making pattern adjustments and selecting compatible fabrics. To accurately determine the yardage you'll need, it's best to purchase your pattern first. After you've made pattern adjustments and eliminated the unnecessary pieces, consult the pattern guide sheet and make a revised layout to determine the amount of fabric to purchase. If you decide to use a large print or plaid fabric that you want to match at the seamlines, you'll need to purchase extra fabric for matching. See Matching Prints & Plaids on page 54.

Garment Pattern Selection

Some commercially available patterns are designed to be reversible, but many others can be adapted. When selecting a pattern, keep in mind the following guidelines.

Fabric type. Read the pattern envelope to make certain the pattern is suitable for the fabric you're considering.

Garment Style. Many garment styles can be reversed. Look for simple design lines with a minimum of seams, darts and details such as pockets or plackets. Patterns without pleats, gathers and other elements that create bulk generally work best. Jackets, vests, ponchos and wrap skirts are especially ideal for reversing, as are pull-on pants and skirts. Patterns designed for fleece fabrics typically have many of these characteristics.

Necklines. Garments without collars are the easiest

to construct and allow for creative bindings and edge finishes. Shawl collars are perfect for garments fabricated with coordinating or contrasting fabrics; the inner side fabric will show when the collar is turned back. Stand up collar styles also work well for reversible garments.

Sleeves. Patterns that are sleeveless or have a dropped shoulder along with raglan or kimono-style sleeves are best for reversible construction techniques. Avoid patterns with set-in sleeves that require easing or fullness in the sleeve cap. Look for plain, cased or turnback cuffs instead of cuffs with plackets.

Closures. Jacket and vest patterns that wrap, zip or meet at the center front are easiest to adapt for reversing. Many jacket and vest patterns that overlap also can be adapted to meet in the center front or for a double-breasted closure (see Garment Pattern Adjustments below). It's best to decide on the closure you want before you begin, as it may effect your edge finish.

Garment Pattern Adjustments

It's easy to adapt a pattern for reversible sewing. Make any standard fitting adjustments such as length first, then modify your pattern as follows:

Omit interfacings and facings. These are unnecessary because each fabric layer finishes and supports the other.

Eliminate the self facing on skirts and pants with elasticized waistline casing, keeping a 5/8" seam allowance above the pattern foldline (Fig. 2.01).

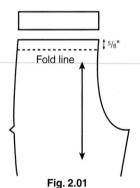

Fig. 2.01
Trim casing self-facing 5/8"
above the pattern fold line.

Eliminate sleeve and lower edge hem allowances, keeping a 5/8" seam allowance. If turn-back cuffs are desired, use pattern tracing cloth to add them to the sleeve length (Fig. 2.02).

For jacket or vest fronts that will have a banded edge, or a tied or laced closure, it's necessary to adjust both front pattern pieces to meet in the center front.

To adapt a buttoned overlap, on each pattern front,

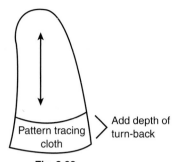

Fig. 2.02
Add turned-back sleeve cuff to
pattern with pattern tracing cloth.

draw a 5/8" seam allowance along the pattern center front marking line; this will be the new cutting line. Trim the excess pattern tissue (Fig. 2.03).

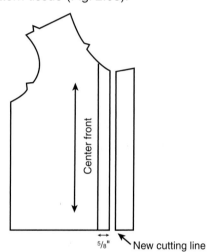

Fig. 2.03
To adjust pattern to meet at center
front, add 5/8" to center front marking
line and cut away excess pattern.

For a jacket or vest front with loop or frog closures, it's necessary to eliminate the right front overlap so the loops will be positioned at the center front.

To adapt a buttoned overlap, keep the left front pattern piece intact. On the right front pattern piece, measure and mark a 5/8" seam allowance along the marked center front line. This will be the new right front cutting line (Fig. 2.04).

To convert a buttoned overlap to a reversible double-breasted overlap, use pattern tracing cloth to add approximately 4" to the center front. Mark the buttonholes on both the right and left fronts (Fig. 2.05)

Fabric Selection

Here's where the fun starts. Keep in mind the purpose of your project as you pick fabrics. If you're combining a business trip and vacation for example, a jacket showcasing a sophisticated fabric on one side for the

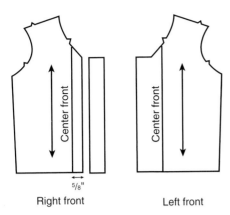

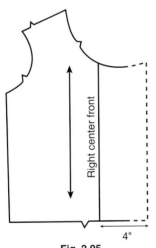

Fig. 2.04
To eliminate a right front overlap, add
⁵⁄₈" to right center front marking line
and cut away excess pattern.
Leave left front intact.

Fig. 2.05
To convert buttoned overlap to
reversible double-breasted overlap,
add 4" to right center front with
pattern tracing cloth.

work day and a fun-loving print on the reverse for evening or sightseeing would be ideal. For the home, projects to change with the seasons are fun to make as well as practical.

You have the choice of using two fabrics for double-layer construction, or one reversible fabric for single-layer construction. Each option has pros and cons to consider as you're perusing fabric choices. As for any sewing project, always consult the pattern envelope for fabric suggestions.

Fabrics for Double-Layer Sewing

For projects constructed with two fabric layers, the fabrics must be compatible in weight, construction and care. Consider these pointers as you shop.

* Fabrics similar in weight and construction—knit or woven—will drape best when placed back-to-back.

Select lightweight, smooth fabrics such as sueded rayon, microfibers, matte jersey, washed or knit silks, and cotton-blend knits for patterns that have a fluid or flowing appearance. Fabrics such as lightweight wool, woven cotton, velvet and linen also work well back-to-back and are suitable for a wide variety of garments where a stiffer appearance is desired. Lighter weights of non-fraying fabrics such as faux suede, fleece and melton offer opportunities for interesting edge finishes on double-layer projects.

* Select opaque fabrics in similar color values to prevent the color or prints showing through the reverse side. Or, for fun, use a lacey, open-weave or sheer fabric on one side with the intention of the reverse fabric showing through. You can also etch your own fabrics to create this same effect (see Artistic Surface Treatments on page 54).

* Combine fabrics that call for similar care. Consider washing and drying, dry-cleaning and pressing requirements. If you combine a dry-clean only fabric with a washable fabric, the garment will need to be dry-cleaned. Pre-wash washable fabrics to prevent uneven shrinking of the completed garment.

Fabrics for Single-Layer Sewing

Reversible fabrics require only a single layer of fabric to construct a reversible project. This category includes double-cloth fabrics—two separate layers of fabric woven or fused together that can be separated, two-faced fabrics—fabrics woven to achieve a different appearance on each side that can't be separated, boiled wool, melton, felted fabrics, sheer fabrics, woven plaids, double-face quilted fabrics, double-face fleece and real or faux suede.

Double-cloth fabrics usually are expensive and aren't as widely available to consumers as other fabrics may be. Most are medium to heavy weight, due to the two separate fabric layers and often used for coats and jackets. These fabrics are most commonly available in wool and wool blends.

Two-face fabrics are more widely available and include jacquards, damask, double knits, satin-back crepe. Fabric weights range from light to heavy.

Double-face quilted fabrics may be the same or different on each side. Boiled wool, melton, felted fabrics, woven plaids, quilted fabrics, fleece and faux suede appear the same on both sides but can be embellished differently to create a reversible garment with two different looks. ✄

Reversible Double-Layer Sewing

Double-layer sewing offers the most versatility for reversible projects. Each side can showcase a different fabric, buttons, pockets and surface embellishments, such as appliqué. For single-layer construction and finishing techniques, see Single-Layer Sewing on page 31.

Whether each layer of your project is pieced or a single piece of fabric, the next step in sewing your reversible project is to decide how you want to assemble the two finished layers. Some projects, such as those with extended fold-over bands, have special requirements that must be made when cutting out the fabric. See Self-Binding Bands on page 26. For most projects, the decision will be whether to assemble layers with right sides facing or wrong sides facing. This will affect whether or not you will leave a seam opening when piecing the layers and also how you will finish the edges. The finished look you want will help you decide.

Double-layer sewing offers the most versatility for reversible projects.

Assembling the layers with the right sides facing will require turning, and is the best option for projects where plain edges, in-seam edge embellishments or handles, and straps or ties are desired. Pull-on skirts or pants and other projects with elasticized casings at the upper edge should be assembled this way.

Assembling the layers with the wrong sides facing eliminates the need for turning and is ideal for projects with edges that will be bound, fringed or serged. Handles, straps or ties will be stitched to the surface after the edges are finished.

Pieced Layer Construction

1. Follow Garment Pattern Adjustments on page 8 to make any necessary pattern adjustments.

2. Follow the pattern or specific project instructions to cut the pattern pieces from fabric. Cut all required garment or project pieces from each of the two fabrics.

3. Stay-stitch the cut edges of the pieces as shown in Fig. 3.01 to make certain both layers retain their original shape.

Fig. 3.01
Stay-stitch cut edges of pattern
pieces. Do not pivot at corners
or backstitch.

4. Apply any desired in-seam edge embellishments. See Seam and Edge Finishes on page 15.

5. Follow the pattern or specific project instructions to sew the sections of each fabric layer together. For projects that will be assembled with the right sides facing, leave a 2"–3" opening for turning in any inside seam of one layer only. See Turning Tips on page 13.

6. Press all seams open after stitching. Trim the corresponding seams of each layer, such as side seams, at different widths as shown in Fig. 3.02. This allows seams to lie smoother when the layers are assembled.

Fig. 3.02
Trim seam allowances at
different widths as shown.

7. Topstitch along each side of the seam line as shown in Fig. 3.03, if desired. This is especially helpful on seam allowances of fabrics that tend to curl or roll up. It's also a nice decorative effect on any fabric.

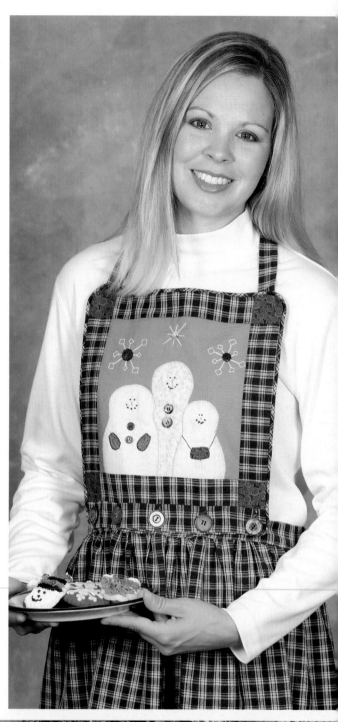

Fig. 3.03
Topstitch along each side
of seam line if desired.

8. To eliminate bulk, avoid placing pockets in the same position on each layer as shown in Fig. 3.04.

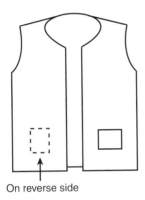

On reverse side

Fig. 3.04
Place pockets in different
positions on each layer.

9. Embellish the edges of each fabric layer with appliqués or trims, if desired.

Right Sides Facing Assembly

When you assemble a project with the right sides facing, you have the options of plain or embellished edge seams, as well as surface edge embellishments. Apply in-seam embellishments, straps and ties to one finished fabric layer only before stitching the layers together.

Turning Tips

Before you sew the layers together, decide how you'll want to turn your project. The best choice depends on what you're making.

For vests, jackets and home decor projects with pieced layers, the least conspicuous place to leave a seam opening is in an inside seam as instructed in Pieced Layer Construction on page 11.

For pillow panels, curtain panels and other projects with layers that are a single piece of fabric, you'll need to leave an opening in an edge seam when sewing the layers together. After you've turned the project, close the opening with a slipstitch.

For handbags and totes, a tricky technique will give

you a finished upper edge and a slipstitched opening in the bottom of one layer. See Special Tips & Techniques on page 54.

Stitching Layers Together

1. Pin the two layers right sides facing, aligning seams and edges.

2. If you're adding a zipper or tie closure to the seam, refer to Closing Time on page 44.

3. If you're adding straps or handles to the seam, sandwich them between the layers, with the raw ends

even with the fabric raw edges as shown in Fig. 3.05.

4. For all pieced-layer projects except pull-on pants or skirts, sew the layers together along all edges. For pillow panels and other non-pieced fabric layers, leave a 2"–3" opening for turning. Trim seam allowances and clip curves.

5. Turn the project right side out through the opening. Close the opening with a slipstitch as shown in Fig. 3.06.

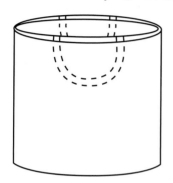

Fig. 3.05
Sandwich straps and handles between bag layers, raw edges aligned.

Fig. 3.06
Close opening with slipstitch.

6. For pull-on pants or skirts, hem the lower edge of each layer separately. Sew the layers together at the waistline only.

7. To keep the layers aligned, hand-tack them together by stitching loosely through the seam line at strategic points. Tack vests and jackets at shoulder and underarm seams; tack pants and skirts at the hem side seams.

8. Edge-stitching or topstitching along the edges will also prevent the layers from shifting.

Seam and Edge Finishes

Edges can be embellished before layers are stitched together with in-seam edge finishes, or after layers are stitched together with sewn or fused surface applications. A vast array of beaded and fabric fringes, colorful ribbons, rickracks and other decorative trims are available, and it's fun to create your own combination of two or more. If you're adding ties or a zipper to an edge, refer to Closing Time on page 44 to apply them before finishing the edge.

In-Seam and Edge Finishes

Purchased fringes, piping and rickrack are attractive in-seam finishes for interior or edge seams. You can also make prairie points, create your own bias binding to cover cord for traditional piping, or create single insertion piping.

Fringe Fun

Fringes are available in materials ranging from leather to feathers. Whether you want to add an air of sophistication or a touch of whimsy, you're sure to find a fringe that will do the job. Before you select one for your project, be sure of its care requirements; some leather and beaded trims need to be dry-cleaned. Two fringes, such as a brush fringe and a ball fringe, can be used together for a creative look. Most are constructed in the same way with the fringe material attached to a header tape to be sewn into the seam. Stitch the fringe to one fabric layer only as follows:

1. Align the fringe header tape edge with the edge seam line. Pin or use double-sided basting tape to secure it in place.

2. Baste the header tape in place slightly inside the seam line.

3. Sew the remaining layer in place along the seam line as shown in Fig. 3.07. Use a zipper foot if the fringe is bulky.

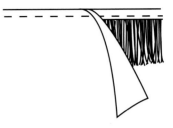

Fig. 3.07
Sew second fabric layer in place as shown.

Cording Cache

Purchased cording adds an attractive finishing touch to home decor projects and is available in a variety of colors in cotton or rayon. Cording with a lip is sewn into an edge seam, while cording without a lip can be used for other elements of a project's design, such as ties. Coordinating colors usually are available to match cording, expanding your design options. To apply cording with a lip to an edge:

1. Pin the cording lip to the fabric edge right side with the cording extending ⅛" beyond the seam line. Clip the lip as necessary to turn corners as shown in Fig. 3.08.

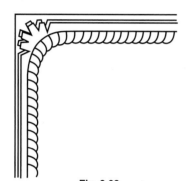

Fig. 3.08
Clip corners of cord lip as necessary
to turn corners smoothly.

2. To join the cording ends invisibly, cut the cord so the ends overlap 3". Remove 2" of the chain-stitching connecting the cord and lip from each cording end. Untwist and overlap the cord ends, twisting them back together as one as shown in Fig. 3.09.

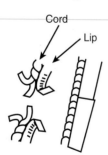

Cord
Lip

Fig. 3.09
Remove stitching connecting lip and
cord at each cord end. Untwist, overlap
and twist together as one.

3. Hand-stitch the joined ends and the lip to the fabric.

4. Sew the remaining layer in place along the seam line using a zipper foot.

Rickrack Ravings

Rickrack is available in a wide range of colors and sizes, from baby to giant. For fun, you can weave two rickrack colors together to create a unique trim as shown in Fig. 3.10.

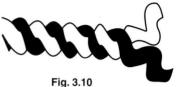

Fig. 3.10
Weave 2 colors of rickrack
together as shown.

Rickrack can be used as a surface application along the edge of each fabric layer, as well as sewn into the seam. To sew it into the seam, center it over the seam line on one fabric layer right side and baste it in place.

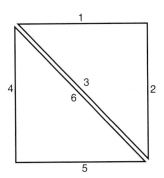

Creating Continuous Bias Binding

The advantage of creating your own bias binding is that your fabric choices are endless, compared to the limited selection of basic colors available for purchase. You can match either of your project layers, or choose a coordinating or contrasting print or solid fabric. It also gives you the option of creating strips in the width you need to cover the cord diameter of your choice. This method ensures straight strips and is quicker than other bias binding cutting and piecing techniques.

1. Determine the bias strip width you want to cut. For binding, double the desired finished width and add 1¼" for seam allowances. To cover piping or cording, wrap a scrap of fabric loosely around the piping or cord and pin it in place as shown in Fig. 3.11. Mark the fabric close to the cord on both sides, remove the fabric and measure between the marks. Add 1¼" to this measure-

ment for seam allowances. The resulting number is the width to cut the strips.

2. To determine the number of bias-strip yards a piece of fabric will yield, multiply the fabric width by the fabric length, then divide this number by the desired cut-strip width. Divide again by 36".

For example, to calculate how many yards of 1½"-wide bias strips an 18" square of fabric will yield, figure it as follows: 18"(width of square) x 18"(length of square) = 324"; 324" divided by 1.5" (cut-strip width) = 216"; 216" divided by 36" (inches per yard) = 6 yards of bias strips.

3. Cut a perfect square; the larger the square, the more strips it will yield. Fold the square in half diagonally and mark the fold line. Cut the square in half along the marked fold line. Place the pieces on a flat surface and number them as shown in Fig. 3.12.

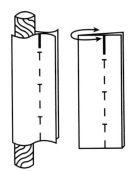

Fig. 3.11
Wrap fabric around cord, pin
and mark. Measure between marks
and add 1¼" for bias strip width.

Fig. 3.12
Number edges of pieces as shown.

4. Use a ¼" seam allowance to sew edges 1 and 5 together with right sides facing. Press the seam open. Place the fabric on a flat surface with the diagonal edges at the sides. Using a clear quilter's ruler and tailor's chalk, begin at one diagonal edge and mark the cut-strip width along the edge as shown in Fig. 3.13. Repeat marking strips across the fabric width. Cut away any excess fabric beyond the final marked line.

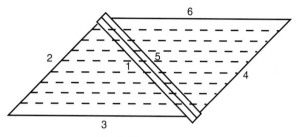

Fig. 3.13
Mark bias strip widths as shown.

5. With right sides facing, offset sides 2 and 4 by one strip-width and stitch the edges together using a ¼" seam allowance; press the seam open. The resulting fabric tube will appear slightly twisted as shown in Fig. 3.14.

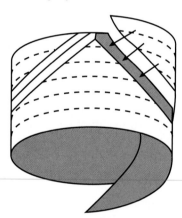

Fig. 3.14
Offset sides 2 and 4 by one strip-width and sew to create a fabric tube.

6. To cut the strips, begin at one offset end and cut continuously along the marked lines to the opposite offset end as shown in Fig. 3.15.

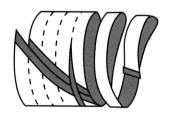

Fig. 3.15
Start at one offset end and cut strips on marked lines as shown.

Traditional Piping

Piping adds design definition and a professional-looking finish to any project. It's created by covering cord or yarn with bias-cut fabric strips. Cord for piping is available in a wide range of sizes, from very small diameters used for intricate details on garments to large cord used for home decor projects.

1. To determine how much piping you will need, measure the seam or seams to be finished.

2. Purchase or create continuous bias-cut fabric strips. The strips should be wide enough to wrap closely around the cord, plus 1¼" for seam allowances, and equal to the desired finished length, plus several inches for an overlap.

3. Adjust the left side of the zipper foot as close to the machine needle as possible. You will be basting the piping layers together ⅛" from the cord, then stitching closer to the cord when applying the piping to the seam line.

4. Wrap the bias strip, wrong sides facing, around the

cord and machine-baste ⅛" from the cord using a zipper foot as shown in Fig. 3.16. The resulting seam allowance should be ½" wide.

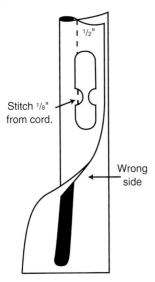

Fig. 3.16
With zipper foot, machine-baste ⅛" from cord.

Piping is stitched to one fabric layer before the seam is stitched. For ease in accurately stitching the piping to the fabric, make certain the piping seam allowance is the same as the fabric seam allowance.

5. Baste the piping to the fabric edge with the piping basting line ⅛" inside the edge seam line and the raw edges even as shown in Fig. 3.17.

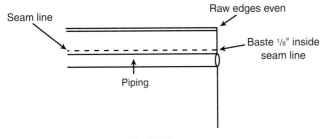

Fig. 3.17
Baste piping to fabric edge, raw edges aligned.

6. To turn outside corners, stop stitching ⅝" from the corner. Clip the piping seam allowance to the stitching line and turn the piping at a 90-degree angle as shown in Fig. 3.18. Continue stitching.

7. For outward curves and corners, clip the piping seam allowance to allow it to spread as shown in Fig. 3.19. For inward curves, clip the piping seam allowance to allow it to overlap. The piping should always lie flat.

8. To join the piping ends, remove the stitching secur-

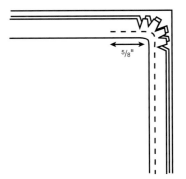

Fig. 3.18
Clip piping seam allowance at outside corners as shown.

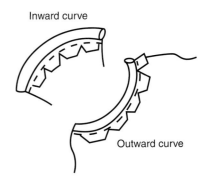

Fig. 3.19
For outward curves, clip piping seam allowance and spread. For inward curves, clip seam allowance and overlap.

ing the piping casing for approximately 2" at the piping end. Cut the cord end to butt the cord beginning, without cutting the casing. Turn under the end of the excess casing and lap it over the piping beginning end as shown in Fig. 3.20.

Fig. 3.20
To join piping ends, cut and butt cord. Overlap casing ends, turning under ½".

9. With right sides facing and the piping sandwiched between the layers, stitch the remaining fabric layer in place along the seam line, using a zipper foot as shown in Fig. 3.21. The previous basting lines should be hidden in the seam allowance.

Single Insertion Piping
Use a rotary cutter and faux suede to make this decorative seam accent.

1. Using a cutting mat, clear quilter's ruler and rotary

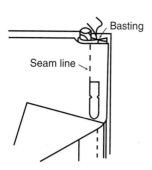

Fig. 3.21
Stitch fabric layers in place along seam line with zipper foot.

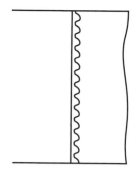

Fig. 3.22
Sandwich decorative trim strip between fabric layers, straight edges aligned, and stitch. Press seam open as shown.

cutter with a straight blade, cut a 1"–1¼"-wide strip of faux suede the length of the seam to be embellished.

2. Replace the rotary cutter straight blade with a decorative blade and trim one strip edge.

3. Sandwich the trim strip between the fabric layers, aligning the straight edge with the fabric edges, and stitch the seam.

Press the seam open as shown in Fig. 3.22.

Prairie Points

Traditionally used for quilting, prairie points make a stunning finish for a jacket, vest or pillow edge. The size of the prairie points is determined by the square or strip width; the smaller size given in the instructions is ideal for garments, but you may want to increase it for larger projects. Practice folding paper samples to determine the size you like.

Following are two techniques for making prairie points. The traditional method of folding fabric squares into triangles can be used to make individual or multiple points. The strip technique will yield a continuous strip of points that is sewn to a flange. The flange makes the strip easier to handle when applying it to the fabric edge. The technique you use is a matter of preference; the end result will have the same appearance.

Traditional Folded Squares

1. Determine how many squares you need to cut to embellish the desired edge. Each prairie point will cover 2½"–3" of the edge.

2. Cut the determined number of 3½" squares from the fabric.

3. Fold each square in half diagonally with the wrong sides facing; press. Fold in half again and press as shown in Fig. 3.23.

Fig. 3.23
Fold prairie point squares in half diagonally and then in half again as shown.

4. Adhere double-sided basting tape to the right side

of the fabric edge to be embellished. Beginning at the center of the edge, align a prairie point raw edge with the fabric edge. Insert the folded corner of the next prairie point into the open side of the first triangle as shown in Fig. 3.24.

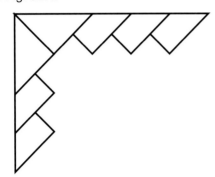

Fig. 3.24
Align raw edges of prairie point with raw edge of fabric, inserting each point into the previous point as shown.

5. Continue to add prairie points along the edge, overlapping them slightly and working from the center out in each direction.

6. Baste the prairie points to the edge.

Folded Strip Prairie Points

1. Determine the length of the prairie-points strip needed to embellish the desired edge.

2. Cut a 4"-wide strip in the determined length. Using tailor's chalk and a clear quilter's ruler, mark the center of the strip vertically and alternate 2" horizontal lines either side of center as shown in Fig. 3.25.

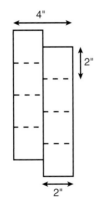

Fig. 3.25
Mark 4" fabric strip as shown. Cut on horizontal lines to center, but do not cut center line.

3. Cut the strip to the center along the marked horizontal lines; do not cut the center line.

4. Fold the points as shown in Fig. 3.26, pressing each point as you fold.

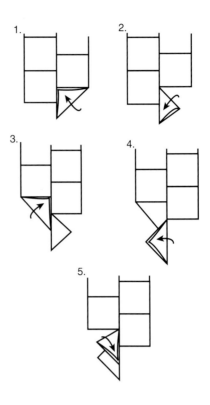

Fig. 3.26
Fold the squares as shown, pressing each point as folded.

5. Overlap and sew the straight edge of the prairie-point strip to the edge of a bias-tape length or a bias-cut fabric strip as shown in Fig. 3.27.

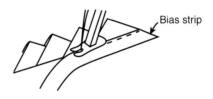

Bias strip

Fig. 3.27
Sew edge of prairie strip to edge of a bias strip as shown.

6. With the bias tape toward the edge, baste the prairie points to the right side of one fabric layer, just inside the seam line. Sew the layers together along the seam line.

Ruffles

Ruffles can add a fun or feminine touch to your reversible project. You can use purchased gathered lace trim or fabric ruffles, or you can make your own. You can make the ruffle with a single fabric to contrast or coordinate with the project fabric layers, or you can make it with a different fabric on each side to match the layers.

Single-Fabric Ruffle

1. To determine the length of the fabric strip needed for a ruffle, multiply the desired finished length by three. For the width, multiply the desired ruffle depth by two and add 1¼" for seam allowances.

2. Cut crosswise or bias fabric strips as determined, piecing strips together if necessary to equal the necessary length.

3. Press the ruffle strip in half lengthwise, wrong sides facing.

4. Stitch two rows of gathering threads, spaced ¼" apart, within the seam allowance as shown in Fig. 3.28.

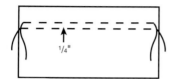

Fig. 3.28
Stitch 2 rows of gathering threads, ¼"
apart, within seam allowance as shown.

5. Pull the bobbin threads to evenly gather the ruffle to the desired length.

6. Pin-mark the ruffle strip and the edge it will be sewn to in fourths. With right sides facing and raw edges

even, match and pin the ruffle to the edge at markings. Distribute the ruffle fullness evenly, then pin in place between the markings as shown in Fig. 3.29.

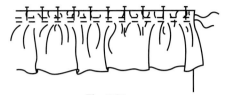

Fig. 3.29
Pin gathered ruffle in place as shown.

7. Sew the ruffle to the edge along the seam line. With right sides facing and the ruffle sandwiched between the layers, stitch the remaining fabric layer in place along the seam line.

Two-Fabric Ruffle

1. To determine the length of the fabric strip needed for a ruffle, multiply the desired finished length by three. Add 1¼" to the desired ruffle depth for the width.

2. Cut crosswise or bias fabric strips from each fabric as determined, piecing strips together if necessary to equal the necessary length.

3. Sew the different-color strips, right sides facing, along one long edge. Turn the strip right side out and press in half lengthwise.

4. Follow the Single-Fabric Ruffle instructions above to finish the ruffle and attach it to the edge.

Surface Edge Finishes

You can add attractive decorative touches to the edges of a garment or project after it's been assembled and turned. It can be as simple as topstitching, or you can apply embellishments with fusible tapes or permanent fabric glue. Keep in mind that any trims that extend beyond the fabric edge will be seen when the project is reversed. It's best to echo the same treatment on the reverse side, or to apply trims, such as decorative ribbons or tapes, that won't be seen from the reverse side.

Wrong Sides Facing Assembly

Assembling projects with wrong sides facing eliminates the need for turning and also offers opportunities for interesting edge finishes.

Stitching Layers Together

1. Pin the two layers wrong sides facing, aligning seams and edges.

2. Baste the layers together along all edges as shown in Fig. 3.30.

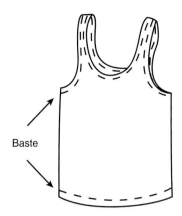

Baste

Fig. 3.30
Wrong sides facing, baste layers together along all edges.

3. To keep the layers aligned, hand-tack them together by stitching loosely through the seam line at strategic points. Tack vests and jackets at shoulder and underarm seams; tack pants and skirts at the hem side seams.

4. Trim the edges evenly, if necessary.

5. If you're adding a zipper or ties for a closure to the edge, refer to Closing Time on page 44.

6. Finish the edges using one of the following options.

Edge Finishes

After the layers are basted together, the edge finish is the final assembly step, as well as a decorative finishing touch. Your choice of edge finishes depends on the effect you want to achieve, as well as the fabric used for the project. Projects sewn with non-fraying fabrics, such as fleece, felt or melton, are ideal for trimmed decorative edges, while a frayed edge may be desired on an even-weave fabric like linen. Bound, banded and serged edges are successful on most fabrics. If you're adding ties or a zipper to an edge, refer to Closing Time on page 44 and apply them before finishing the edge.

Binding

Binding is the most basic technique for finishing raw edges. It's a neat and practical way to encase the edge and is also an attractive accent in a contrasting color. You can cut a bias strip from woven fabric (see Creating Continuous Bias Binding on page 17) or cut decorative binding from fleece or suede. You can also use purchased folded bias tape, quilt binding, braid or grosgrain ribbon. Spandex trim strips are especially ideal for finishing fleece edges. See Specialty Fabrics on page 40.

Cutting and Applying Bias Strips

To cut and apply your own bias strips:

1. Cut bias or knit fabric strips four times the desired finished width (ususally ¼") of the binding and piece them to equal the length of the edge to be bound, plus 2". Lightly press the strip in half lengthwise, wrong sides facing, being careful not to stretch. Open the binding and lightly press the lengthwise edges, wrong sides facing, to meet in the center as shown in Fig. 3.31, again being careful not to stretch the fabric.

2. To prepare an edge for binding, mark the seam line and cut away the seam allowance. The binding center fold will be at the edge when it's completed.

3. Open one binding fold and turn back one short end.

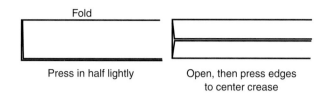

Fold

Press in half lightly

Open, then press edges to center crease

Fig. 3.31
Press bias strip in half lengthwise. Open and bring raw edges to center fold as shown; press.

With right sides facing and the bias strip on top, beginning at the turned-back end, pin the binding to the edge, aligning the edges. Overlap the starting end and trim any excess binding length as shown in Fig. 3.32.

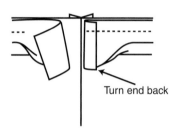

Turn end back

Fig. 3.32
Overlap ends of binding, folding back one short end as shown.

4. Sew the binding to the edge along the upper fold line as shown in Fig. 3.33. Follow Mitering Binding on Outer Corners below to miter any corners.

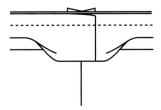

Fig. 3.33
Sew binding to fabric along upper fold line
as shown, overlapping folded back end.

5. Press the seam allowances toward the binding. Fold the binding in half on the center pressed line; it should be at the fabric edge and the remaining pressed edge should still be turned under as shown in Fig. 3.34.

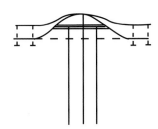

Fig. 3.34
Fold binding in half at fabric edge. Turn
remaining pressed edge under and
pin in place close to edge.

6. By hand, slipstitch the remaining binding edge to the fabric or topstitch close to the edge.

To apply purchased bias binding, follow the same instructions above.

Applying Braid or Grosgrain Ribbon
1. Follow step 2 above to cut away the seam allowances.

2. Press the braid or ribbon in half lengthwise. Wrap the braid or ribbon over the fabric edge as shown in Fig. 3.35. Pin or use double-sided basting tape to secure. Follow Mitering Binding on Outer Corners to miter any corners.

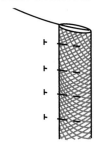

Fig. 3.35
Wrap folded braid or ribbon over fabric
edge as shown and pin in place.

3. Topstitch close to the edge, being careful to catch the binding edge on each side.

Cutting and Applying Decorative Binding
Cut decorative binding from faux suede or fleece to bind the edges of like projects. Fleece is best used to bind fleece projects, but faux suede is an attractive binding for wools and other fabrics as well as faux suede.

1. Following the instructions in Frayed Not on page 27, use a decorative blade to cut binding strips twice the desired finished binding width. Cut fleece on the crosswise grain.

2. Fold the binding around the fabric edge and topstitch it in place ¼" from the decorative edge as shown in Fig. 3.36.

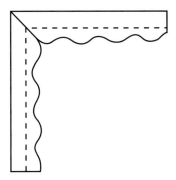

Fig. 3.36
Topstitch trim in place ¼"
from the decorative edge.

Mitering Binding on Outer Corners
1. To miter binding on an outer corner, stitch toward the corner and stop ¼"—or the finished binding width—from the corner; backstitch to secure the stitching and cut threads.

2. Fold the binding away from the garment diagonally and press. Fold the binding back toward the garment, aligning the fold with the edge as shown in Fig. 3.37. Resume stitching, securing stitches at the beginning.

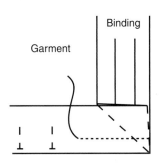

Fig. 3.37
Fold binding away from garment
and then back toward it, aligning
the fold with the edge.

3. Press the seam flat and fold the binding over the raw edge, forming a miter at the corner. Be sure to keep the corner square. Form a mitered corner on the reverse side when you slipstitch it in place as shown in Fig. 3.38.

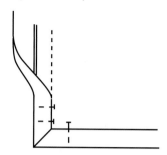

Fig. 3.38
Fold binding over the raw edge and to the reverse side, forming a mitered corner.

Banding

Banding creates an extension of the edge. It's ideal to use for garment hems, front closures that have been adapted to meet in the center (see Garment Pattern Adjustments on page 8) and the edges of home decor table and window treatments. Choose a banded edge finish for a garment front if you want to use in-seam buttonholes and add the buttonholes as you apply the band. See Closing Time on page 44.

1. Determine the desired band width and add 1¼" for seam allowances to the measurement. Cut and piece strips this width to equal the edge length, plus 2".

2. Press the band in half lengthwise with wrong sides facing. Open the fold and fuse interfacing to one lengthwise half between the fold and the seam allowance. With right sides facing and edges aligned, stitch the band to the garment edge as shown in Fig. 3.39.

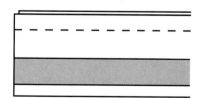

Fig. 3.39
Fuse interfacing to lengthwise half of band. Right sides facing, raw edges aligned, stitch to garment edge as shown.

3. Press the seam allowance toward the band. Fold the band to the reverse side and press the seam allowance under.

4. To miter outer banding corners, stop stitching ⅝" from the corner; secure stitches and cut threads. Diagonally fold the banding out. From the banding

center fold line, measure twice the banding finished width and mark as shown in Fig. 3.40.

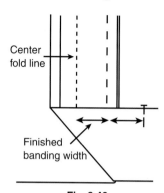

Fig. 3.40
Fold band diagonally away from garment. From band center fold line measure distance equal to twice the width of the finished band and mark that point as shown.

5. Fold the banding straight back at the mark and pin it to the adjacent edge. Begin at the fold and continue stitching as shown in Fig. 3.41. Press the seam flat.

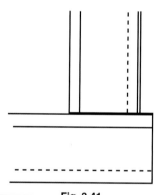

Fig. 3.41
Fold band back at mark and pin to adjacent edge. Stitch along band fold line; press.

6. Form a miter at the corner, then fold the banding to the reverse side and form a miter at the reverse corner. Slipstitch or topstitch the edge in place as shown in Fig. 3.42.

Self-Binding Bands

The self-binding band is actually a binding that creates a banded look on one side and a plain edge with a zigzag stitching border on the reverse side. It's especially useful for straight garment edges and the edges of table linens and window treatments.

1. When cutting out the fabric layers, cut one layer without seam allowances on the edges to be bound, and the other layer 1½"–2" wider than the other on the edges to be bound.

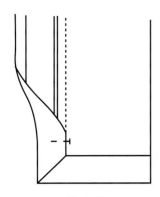

Fig. 3.42
Form miter on right side of garment,
then fold band to reverse side and form
a miter; slipstitch fold in place.

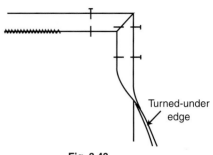

Fig. 3.43
Turn under ½" on larger fabric layer.
Bring to front fabric layer and pin as shown.

2. Place the layers, wrong sides facing, with the larger layer on the bottom and the edge extending evenly. On projects like napkins, you will center the smaller layer on the larger layer.

3. Press under ½" on the extended edges, then fold the extended band around the edge and pin in place as shown in Fig. 3.43.

4. Stitch the edges in place using a narrow zigzag stitch.

Fray Frenzy

Fabrics such as linen, linen blends, some cottons and other fabrics that fray evenly are ideal for creating a self-fabric fringed edge. Look for fabric with a moderate to loose weave and test a swatch first to determine how well it frays.

1. Stitch a narrow zigzag stitch along the edge seam line, stitching over the basting stitches.

2. Cut to the stitching line at 2" intervals along the length of the edge.

3. Use a pin or needle to remove the horizontal threads between the cuts to make fringe as shown in Fig. 3.44.

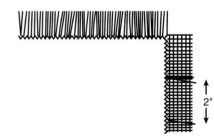

Fig. 3.44
Remove horizontal threads between
cuts to make fringe as shown.

Frayed Not

On the other end of the fabric spectrum, non-fraying fabrics are also perfect candidates for creative edge-finishing techniques. Consider these techniques for leather, suede, fleece, felt, medium-weight wool melton or boiled-wool projects.

Buttonhole Stitch

1. Restitch the basted seam lines using a regular-length machine stitch appropriate for your selected fabric.

2. Use a large-eye tapestry needle and

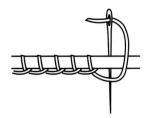

Fig. 3.45
Buttonhole stitch.

pearl cotton or yarn to stitch a
buttonhole stitch around the edge
as shown in Fig. 3.45.

Decorative Trim

1. Restitch the basted seam lines
using a regular-length machine stitch
appropriate for your selected fabric.

2. If desired, fuse the seam allowances with fusible-web tape or permanent fabric glue.

3. Use one or more of the following
tools to trim the seam allowances in
a decorative pattern or embellish
them with a design.

• Decorative-edge fabric scissors
  are available in a variety of
  shapes ranging from pinking
  to waves.

• Rotary cutters with decorative blades are available
  in a variety of shapes. Work on a rotary-cutting mat
  and use the cutter with a clear quilter's ruler to trim
  the edges.

• Use leather punches and a mallet to punch designs
  in suede or faux suede. These and decorative
  paper punches can be used on other thin, compact
  fabrics such as some felts. Test for success on a
  scrap of fabric.

To punch a design, place the suede on a punching
board. Hold the punch perpendicular to the surface
and hit the punch top firmly with the mallet. Use one
or more punch shapes to randomly punch designs
around the stamped border.

Serger Style

If you have a serger, you probably know it's wonderful
for finishing seams and edges, and thanks to today's
decorative threads, there are many options for decorative effects. Serging is also an easy way to finish the
edges of knit garments with ribbing.

Threads

Each of these threads results in a unique look that
varies depending on the type of fabric being serged.
It's best to test on scraps of fabric first.

• Crochet thread is slightly thicker than topstitching
  thread. It can be used in both loopers, but not in
  the needle.

• Metallic threads vary with the brand. Some are only
  suitable in the upper looper and may fray in the
  lower looper or the needle. Good for decorative
  rolled edges.

• Pearl cotton is a loosely twisted thread that is
  shiny and soft. It's best used in the upper looper
  and may snag when used in the lower looper.

• Rayon thread is used primarily in the upper looper.
  It adds an attractive sheen to an edge. It tends to
  break when used in the lower looper, and is best
  used for a rolled edge on reversible projects.

• Ribbon used for knitting is soft and ¼" wide or less.
  It can be used in the upper looper.

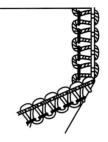

Fig. 3.46
Loops should meet on the
fabric edge as shown.

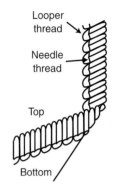

Looper
thread

Needle
thread

Top

Bottom

Fig. 3.47
Upper looper thread should
completely wrap the fabric
edge as shown.

- Serger thread is an all-purpose thread and can be used in both loopers and the needle. Depending on the fabric, you can shorten the stitch length for more coverage or lengthen it for an open look.

- Topstitching thread is a highly twisted, heavier thread and can be used in both loopers and the needle. It provides better coverage than regular thread.

- Woolly Nylon™ thread, from Y.L.I., adds a fuzzy appearance to an edge and provides excellent coverage. It can be used in both loopers and the needle. Loosen the tensions to allow it to flow smoothly.

- Yarn that is fine with an even, tight twist can be used. Make certain it doesn't break easily. Use it in the upper looper only.

Stitches

A balanced three-thread overlock stitch looks the same on both sides when the same thread in used in the upper and lower loopers. The loops should meet at the fabric edge as shown in Fig. 3.46.

Some heavy decorative threads are suitable for the

upper looper only, but don't let that discourage you from using them as a reversible edge finish. Loosen the upper looper tension and tighten the lower looper tension so the decorative thread completely wraps the edge as shown in Fig. 3.47.

For a rolled edge, use rayon, silk or metallic threads to add a decorative shimmer, or Woolly Nylon™ to add texture.

Create a lettuce-leaf edging on lightweight stretchy knits. Use a rolled edge set on a short satin-stitch length as shown in Fig. 3.48.

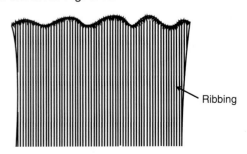

Ribbing

Fig. 3.48
Create a lettuce-leaf edging
with a short satin stitch.

Straps and Handles

Add straps and handles to the surface of the assembled garment or project.

1. Follow the tie instructions in Closing Time on page 44 to make straps or handles in the desired width, or use purchased strapping trim.

2. Turn the strap or handle raw ends under and topstitch them in place.

3. Position the ends on the garment or project and securely stitch in place as shown in Fig. 3.49.

4. If desired, cut a small wedge of faux suede or leather and stitch for each strap or handle end. Position and stitch it over the handle end to cover as shown in Fig. 3.50. ✄

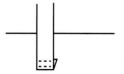

Fig. 3.49
Stitch handles securely
in place as shown.

Fig. 3.50
Stitch a small wedge of faux suede or
leather over each handle end as shown.

Reversible Single-Layer Sewing

Single-layer sewing is a great way to show-case double-cloth or double-face fabrics, sheer fabrics, reversible quilted fabrics, heavyweight wool (such as melton), heavy-weight felt, fleece, leather and suede. Any fabric that has two attractive sides and enough body can be used. It's also the most practical technique for very heavy fabrics that don't lend themselves well to facings and seam allowances.

Because there's no way to hide seam allowance, pockets and other construction elements as in double-layer sewing, it's necessary to use specialty sewing tech-niques that look attrac-tive on both sides. You can also choose to use facings and hems as edge fin-ishes on suitable fabrics, then topstitch them in place as a decorative element.

Many of these techniques are applicable to garment sewing, but quite a few, such as seam and edge finishes, are also ideal for sewing home decor projects.

While this may sound like a challenge at first, it's actu-ally the fun—and decorative—part, and affords numer-ous options for creativity.

Although these fabrics don't really have a right or wrong side, they will be referred to as such for clarity in the following instructions. Many of these techniques are applicable to garment sewing, but quite a few, such as seam and edge finishes, are also ideal for sewing home decor projects.

Cutting and Construction

1. Follow Garment Pattern Adjustments on page 8 to make any necessary pattern adjustments. If you want to use flat-felled seams on heavy fabrics, cut the seam allowances slightly wider to provide extra fabric for turning under.

2. If desired, you can use neckline or armhole facings and make them part of the design by cutting them in a contrasting fabric or color.

3. Make pattern markings with chalk, pins or other marking materials that are easily removed.

4. Follow the pattern or specific project instructions to cut the pattern pieces from fabric.

5. To add zipped or tied closures, see Closing Time on page 44.

6. Construct the garment or project following the specific instructions and referring to the following instructions to finish darts, seams and edges, and to add extras such as collars or pockets. Refer to the special leather, suede and fleece instructions on page 40 to work with these fabrics.

Seam Style

The best seaming technique to use depends on sever-al factors: the fabric weight, garment style, seam loca-tion and desired finished effect. Some seam finishes are not appropriate for seam shapes and locations, so you may use more than one for a garment.

Because most of the seam allowances will be seen, take extra care when stitching to ensure that the widths are uniform within each seam and from one seam to another. Neat and even topstitching is also necessary to achieve professional-looking results with these seam finishes.

Woven Fabric Seams

Bound Seams
Depending on the look you wish to achieve, you can trim the seam allowances before binding for a narrow trim effect, or bind the entire ⅝" width for a wider trim look. Use bias strips, ribbon or braid for binding.

1. Stitch the seam with right sides facing. Press the seam open, then press it to one side. Trim the seam allowances to the desired width. The seam allowance should be completely covered by the binding.

2. Press under the raw edges if using bias strips. Press the binding in half lengthwise with wrong sides facing.

3. Encase the seam allowances in the binding and stitch close to the edge as shown in Fig. 4.01.

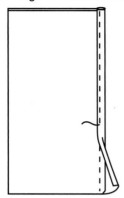

Fig. 4.01
Encase the seam allowance with binding
and stitch close to the edge as shown.

4. Press the bound seam allowance to one side and edge-stitch along the fold as shown in Fig. 4.02.

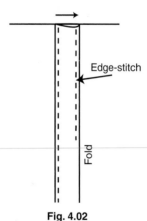

Edge-stitch

Fold

Fig. 4.02
Press the bound seam allowance to one
side and edge-stitch along the fold.

Edge-Stitched Seams

This seam finish works best on light- to medium-weight fabrics. It adds a contrasting trim effect because the fabric from the reverse side shows on the seam allowances.

1. Stitch the seam with wrong sides together. Press the seam open.

2. Press each seam allowance edge under ⅛".

3. Edge-stitch each folded edge to the garment as shown in Fig. 4.03.

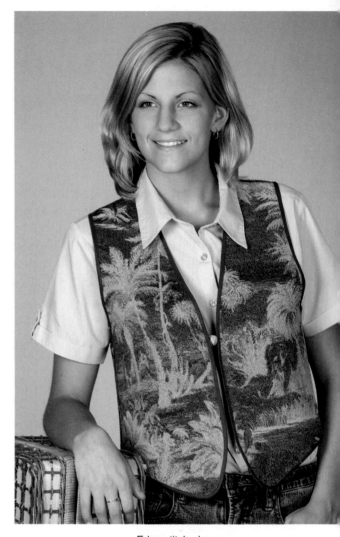

Edge-stitched seam

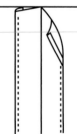

Fig. 4.03
Press seam allowance edges under ⅛"
and edge-stitch each folded edge to the
garment.

Flat-Felled Seam

Use this classic seam finish for straight seams. It's especially suitable for lighter fabric weights, is very sturdy and offers a polished finished look that's nice on both sides. The finished seam will match the fabric.

1. Stitch the seam with wrong sides facing. Press the seam open, then press both seam allowances to one side.

2. Trim the lower seam allowance to ⅛".

3. Press under ¼" along the edge of the upper seam allowance.

4. Edge-stitch the seam allowance to the garment close to the folded edge as shown in Fig. 4.04.

French Seam

This is the classic seam for sheer fabrics; it looks nicest if the finished width is ¼" or less, and it's used on straight or slightly curved seams. It's a self-finished seam in which all raw edges are enclosed. The seam is stitched twice—once from the right side and again from the wrong side.

1. Stitch the seam with wrong sides facing, using a ⅜" seam allowance.

2. Trim the seam allowances to ⅛" and press the seam open.

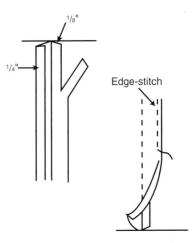

Fig. 4.04
Trim the under seam allowance to ⅛".
Press under ¼" along the edge of
upper seam allowance. Edge-stitch the
upper seam allowance to the garment
close to the folded edge.

3. Fold the right sides together, with the stitched seam exactly on the edge of the fold; press. The seam line is now ¼" from the fold. Stitch along the seam line as shown in Fig. 4.05.

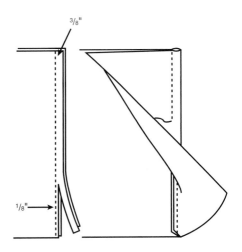

Fig. 4.05
Wrong sides facing, stitch a ⅜" seam;
trim to ⅛" and press open. Fold right
sides together with stitched seam
exactly on the edge of the fold; press.
Stitch along the seam line as shown.

4. Press the seam to one side. Edge-stitch in place as shown in Fig. 4.06.

Fringed Seam

This seam finish adds a casual, fun look and is appropriate for straight seams on loosely woven fabrics. The fringe will only show on one side of the garment; the other side will appear as a topstitched seam.

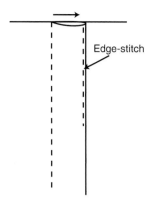

Edge-stitch

Fig. 4.06
Press seam to one side and edge-stitch
in place as shown.

1. Stitch the seam with wrong sides facing, using a
⅜" seam allowance. Press the seam flat, then press
it open.

2. Trim the lower seam allowance to ⅛". Press the
upper seam allowance over it.

3. Stitch the seam allowances in place ¼" from the
seam line. Clip the free seam allowance to the stitching line at 1" intervals and ravel the threads as shown
in Fig. 4.07.

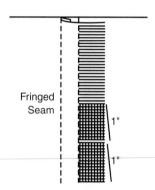

Fringed
Seam

1"

1"

Fig. 4.07
Clip free seam allowance to the
stitching at 1" intervals and ravel
threads as shown.

Taped Seam

Similar to a bound seam, but less bulky, the raw
edges of the seam allowance are covered with a flat
braid or bias binding. It can be used on any seam
shape or type of fabric. Choose trim to match the fabric, or a contrasting trim for a more decorative look.

1. Stitch the seam with wrong sides facing. Press the
seam open.

2. Trim the seam allowances so they are narrower
than the width of the braid.

3. Place the braid over the trimmed seam and stitch

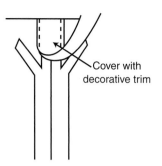

Cover with
decorative trim

Fig. 4.08
Trim seam allowance. Place decorative trim over
seam and stitch close to edges.

close to both braid edges as shown in Fig. 4.08.

Non-Fraying Fabric Seams

Most non-fraying fabrics, such as fleece, felt, leather and
suede, can be seamed like woven fabrics, but their char-

acteristics also make them suitable for alternative seam finishes. Depending on the fabric, these finishes often help reduce bulk and provide an attractive finishing touch.

Consult Specialty Fabrics on page 40 for special considerations, such as finger-pressing instead of using an iron for some of these fabrics.

Lapped Seam

This overlapping seam is ideal for heavy, non-fraying fabrics. It reduces bulk and results in a flat, smooth seam. Depending on the garment you're constructing, lap top over bottom, front over back, center over side or armholes over sleeves. You can also add a decorative edge to the seam allowance.

1. If desired, use decorative-edge scissors or a rotary cutter with a decorative blade to trim the edge that will be on top.

2. With right sides up, overlap the edges to be seamed 1¼", or twice the seam allowance. Secure the overlapped edges with self-adhesive, double-sided basting tape.

3. Stitch ¼", then ½" from the edge as shown in Fig. 4.09.

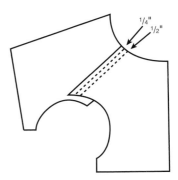

Fig. 4.09
Stitch ¼", then ½" from edge as shown.

Mock Flat-Felled Seam

This is a variation of the Flat-Felled Seam used for woven fabrics.

1. Sew the seam with right sides facing.

2. Trim one seam allowance to ⅛" as shown in Fig. 4.10.

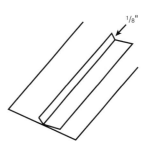

Fig. 4.10
Trim one seam allowance to ⅛".

3. Press the remaining seam allowance over the trimmed one and topstitch it in place ¼" from the seam line as shown in Fig. 4.11.

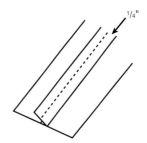

Fig. 4.11
Press untrimmed seam allowance over trimmed and topstitch in place ¼" from seam line.

4. Trim the excess seam allowance close to the top-stitching.

Topstitched Seam Allowances

This is a variation on the edge-stitch finish used for woven fabrics.

1. Sew a regular seam with right sides facing.

2. Press the seam open.

3. Topstitch each seam allowance ¼" from the seam line as shown in Fig. 4.12.

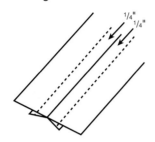

Fig. 4.12
Topstitch each seam allowance ¼"
from seam.

4. Trim the excess seam allowance close to the top-stitching.

5. For a variation, evenly trim the seam allowances with decorative-edge scissors or a rotary cutter with a decorative blade and topstitch close to the edge as shown in Fig. 4.13.

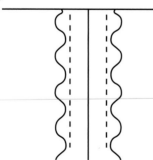

Fig. 4.13
Trim seam allowances with decorative blade
and topstitch close to edges as shown.

Decorative Details

With any project, decorative details can make a big difference. Combine practicality with creativity and turn darts, facings, pockets and collar attachments into design expressions.

Darts

If darts are necessary for your garment, you can turn them into a decorative element.

1. Stitch the dart as usual.

2. Press the dart flat and topstitch the edge as shown in Fig. 4.14.

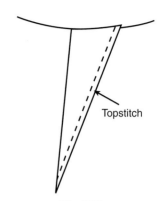

Fig. 4.14
Press dart flat and topstitch the edge
as shown.

Facings

Rather than eliminating facings, you can choose to use them as decorative edge finishes for single-layer reversible garments. Use matching or contrasting fabric, depending on the look you want to achieve.

1. Follow the pattern guide sheet and stitch the facing to the edge with right sides facing.

2. Turn the facing to the wrong side. For woven fabrics, turn under and topstitch the facing raw edge.

3. Topstitch the facing close to the edge as shown in Fig. 4.15.

Fig. 4.15
Topstitch facings close to edges
as shown.

Pockets

Patch pockets are the most practical pocket application for single-layer garments, although you can use an in-seam pocket if you want to topstitch it in place on the reverse side. You can dress up a basic patch pocket by adding a flap to its upper edge or a welt to the reverse side. Other options, such as edges trimmed with a decorative rotary-cutter blade or scissors are ideal for non-fraying fabrics.

Basic Patch Pocket

Woven Fabrics

1. Cut the desired size patch pocket from fabric, adding ½" side and 1½" upper edge seam allowances.

2. Finish the allowances with serging or zigzag stitching. Press under the side and lower edge seam allowances, then the upper edge seam allowance.

3. Position the pocket on the garment and secure it with pins, double-sided basting tape or fusible-web tape.

4. Stitch the pocket in place along the side and lower edges.

5. Reinforce the upper edges of the corners with zigzag stitches, backstitches or reinforcement triangles as shown in Fig. 4.16.

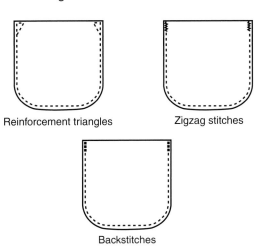

Reinforcement triangles   Zigzag stitches

Backstitches

Fig. 4.16
Reinforce upper pocket edges with reinforcement triangles, zigzag stitches or backstitches.

Non-fraying Fabrics

1. Use scissors or a rotary cutter with a straight or decorative blade to cut out the pocket. Eliminate side and lower edge seam allowances and add a 1" seam allowance to the upper edge.

2. Turn under and pin the upper edge seam allowance.

3. Follow steps 3 through 5 for Woven Fabrics to complete the pocket.

Patch Pocket With Flap

1. Follow the Basic Patch Pocket instructions for the appropriate fabric to cut out the pocket, adding 1"–2" to the upper edge for the flap.

2. Refer to Edge Finishes on page 39, and finish the pocket edges with the technique of your choice.

3. Position the pocket on the garment and secure it with pins, double-sided basting tape or fusible-web tape.

4. Stitch the pocket in place along the side and lower edges, leaving the flap free as shown in Fig. 4.17.

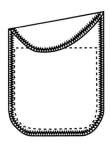

Fig. 4.17
Topstitch pocket in place along side and lower edges, leaving flap free as shown.

5. Follow step 5 for Woven Fabrics to reinforce the ends of the stitching.

6. Fold the flap down.

Patch Pocket With Reverse-Side Welt or Flap
This pocket style has a pocket opening covered with a welt or flap on one side and a patch pocket covering the opening on the reverse side. The flap is attached to the garment above the pocket opening; the welt is attached below the pocket opening.

1. Mark the pocket opening on the garment.

2. Baste around the marked opening ½" from the edge and ends. Carefully cut the opening, cutting slits to the basting corners as shown in Fig. 4.18.

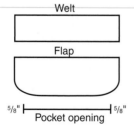

Fig. 4.18
Baste around marked pocket opening ¹/₂"
from edge and ends. Carefully cut the
opening and slit to the corners as shown.

3. Turn the opening edges to the wrong side and slip-stitch them in place.

4. Cut a rectangular welt or curved flap from fabric, adding seam allowances. The welt or flap finished length should be 1¼" longer than the pocket opening as shown in Fig. 4.19.

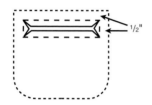

Fig. 4.19
Cut rectangular or curved flap 1¹/₄"
longer than pocket opening.

5. See Edge Finishes on page 39 to turn under and topstitch both short edges and one long edge of the welt or flap, mitering the corners.

6. Right sides facing, center and stitch the flap raw edge to the garment above the opening or the welt raw edge to the garment below the opening as shown in Fig. 4.20.

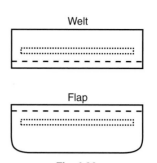

Fig. 4.20
Stitch welt raw edge to garment below
opening or flap raw edge to garment
above opening.

7. Fold the flap down and slipstitch the upper corners to the garment, or fold the welt up and slipstitch the ends to the garment as shown in Fig. 4.21

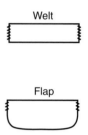

Fig. 4.21
Fold welt up and slipstitch ends to
garment. Fold flap down and slipstitch
upper corners to garment.

8. Make the desired patch pocket at least 1" larger than the pocket opening, following the instructions on page 37. Apply it to the reverse garment side, covering the opening and any flap or welt stitching lines as shown in Fig. 4.22

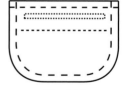

Fig. 4.22
Apply patch pocket to reverse side of
garment, covering opening and any flap
or welt stitching lines.

Collars

Shawl, stand-up, notched and ribbed collars are all suitable for a reversible single-layer garment. The best choice depends on the look you want—some of these versions will have a visible seam edge on one side of the garment.

Shawl Collar
Shawl collars are seamless and easiest to create for a

reversible single-layer neckline because they are part of the garment fronts.

1. Follow the pattern instructions to construct the garment.

2. Refer to Edge Finishes on this page and finish the collar and front opening edges in a continuous step as shown in Fig. 4.23.

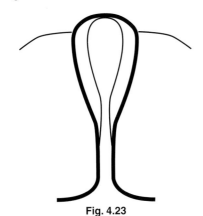

Fig. 4.23
Finish collar and front opening edges as shown.

Notched Collar

1. Refer to Edge Finishes on this page. Finish the collar outer raw edges.

2. Attach the collar raw edge to the neckline as you finish the neckline raw edge as shown in Fig. 4.24.

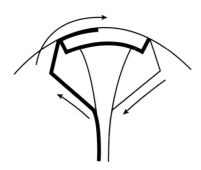

Fig. 4.24
Finish garment front opening edges as
you sew collar in place.

Stand-up Collars

Stand-up collars can be attached using an overlapped edge or an insertion technique. The insertion technique requires two layers of fabric.

Overlapped Edge

An overlapped edge is the best stand-up collar application for heavyweight or bulky fabrics. It can also be used for lighter-weight fabrics, but you will first need to make the collar with two layers of fabric for stability, interfacing it if necessary.

1. Refer to Edge Finishes on this page to finish the garment neckline edge and the collar outer edges.

2. For lighter-weight fabric, sew the two collar layers together along the outer edges with right sides facing. Trim the seam allowances, turn the collar right side out and press the seam. Baste the lower raw edges together.

3. Pin the collar to the neckline with the edges overlapping. Stitch the collar in place close to the neckline edge and again close to the collar edge as shown in Fig. 4.25.

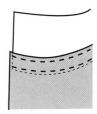

Fig. 4.25
Overlap collar and neckline. Stitch
close to neckline edge and again close
to collar edge as shown.

Insertion Collar

The insertion collar is suitable for all fabrics. Interfacing may be desired for lighter weights.

1. For heavyweight fabrics, sew the collar layers together with wrong sides facing, and leaving the lower edge open. Refer to Edge Finishes on this page to finish the outer edges.

2. For medium and lighter fabric weights, sew the collar layers together with right sides facing and leaving the lower edge open. Trim the seam allowances, turn the collar right side out and press the seam.

3. Trim the neckline and collar raw edge seam allowances to ¼".

4. Turn under each collar edge seam allowance and topstitch ⅛" from the edge. Do not stitch the seam allowances together.

5. Insert the garment neckline edge into the open collar edge and pin in place as shown in Fig. 4.26.

6. Baste the collar to the neckline, being careful to catch both layers of the collar. Permanently stitch it in place, stitching close to the collar lower edge. Remove the basting stitches.

Edge Finishes

Edge finishes are more limited for single-layer sewing than for double-layer sewing, because there aren't any

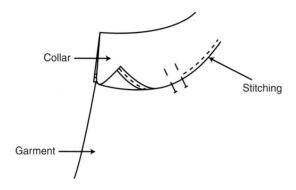

Fig. 4.26
Insert garment neckline into open collar
edge and pin in place.

Fig. 4.27
Pull away threads between clips as
shown.

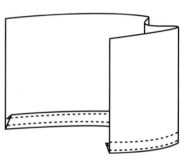

Fig. 4.28
Press raw edge under ¼" and again
³/₈". Topstitch close to garment edge
and again ¼" from edge as shown.

seams for insertion. However, you do have multiple edge-finishing choices, depending on the garment style and the fabric.

Many of these options are the same as those used for double-layer garments assembled with wrong sides facing. Bound, banded, frayed, decorative no-fray and serged techniques are equally suitable for finishing single-layer edges. Refer to them beginning on page 24. Also see Surface Edge Finishes on page 23 for additional options. If you're adding ties or a zipper to an edge, refer to Closing Time on page 44 to apply them before finishing the edge.

Ravel Fringe

Depending on the fabric, you can achieve a variety of looks with this technique. Do not use it for loosely woven fabrics that will ravel completely. Experiment first with scraps of your fabric to determine the result. For example, cut edges of knits will curl under, denims will ravel on the edges only, and non-fraying fabrics will remain intact.

1. Staystitch along the seam line of each edge to be finished.

2. Determine the fringe depth and trim the seam allowance if necessary.

3. Clip to staystitching at ¾" intervals and pull away threads between clips as shown in Fig. 4.27.

Topstitched Edge

This finish can be used for all but the heaviest fabrics.

Light- to Medium-Weight Fabric
1. Press the raw edge of the fabric under ¼", then press it under ⅜" again.

2. Topstitch close to the garment edge, and again ¼" from the edge as shown in Fig. 4.28.

Heavy-Weight Fabric

1. Trim the seam allowances to ½".

2. Serge the raw edges or finish them with zigzag stitches.

3. Press the seam allowance to the wrong side.

4. Topstitch close to each edge of the seam allowance as shown in Fig. 4.29.

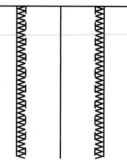

Fig. 4.29
Topstitch close to edge of seam
allowance as shown.

Specialty Fabrics

Specialty fabrics, such as suede, fleece and velvet, are wonderful for a variety of reversible projects. However, these fabrics also have some unique characteristics and requirements for successful sewing. Keep in mind the following tips for each of these fabrics when working with them.

Suede

Suede—real or faux—is wonderful to work with, requires no edge finishing and is easily cut and embellished. Keep the following considerations in mind for achieving professional-looking results. Suede is best used for single-layer sewing, especially in heavier weights.

Don't fold suede. Roll yardage up with tissue paper to prevent creases and hang garments.

Needles and pins will damage suede. Pin in the seam allowances only, or use double-sided self-adhesive basting tape to secure layers. Use chalk to mark pattern markings.

Use a needle for leather in your sewing machine. Set the stitch length at 8–19 stitches per inch. Be careful not to stretch the fabric as you sew.

Never press suede with an iron. Finger-press seam allowances open. Apply fabric glue to seam allowance

wrong sides and roll the seam flat with a brayer while the glue is wet as shown in Fig. 4.30.

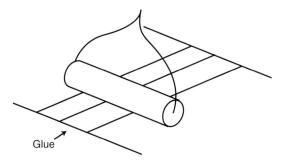

Fig. 4.30
Glue suede seams flat and roll with a brayer.

Stamping and stenciling are fun ways to embellish suede and can be used on both fabric sides. See Special Tips & Techniques on page 54. Apply these designs before stitching seams in the area to be embellished.

Suede edges are easily trimmed with a rotary cutter

and a plain or decorative blade. See Frayed Not on page 27 for edge finishes.

Fleece

Fleece fabrics are widely available in a variety of prints and solid colors. Their unique characteristics make them easy to work with, warm, and a favorite fabric for adults and children as well. Due to its bulk, it's best to use a single layer of double-face fleece for reversible sewing.

Cutting

Use a "with nap" pattern layout, even if there isn't an obvious nap to the fleece. This avoids having pieces within the garment appear to be different.

Always mark the "right" or same side of all pieces to avoid confusion during construction.

Use a single-layer pattern layout if the fleece is especially thick.

Construction

The synthetic fibers of fleece will dull sewing machine needles. Begin each project with a new size 12/80 needle.

Use a stitch length of 7–9 stitches per inch for accessories and looser-fitting garments, or 12–14 stitches per inch for closer-fitting garments. A too-short stitch length may distort the seam by stretching the fleece.

Serged, topstitched seam allowances and mock fell seams are the best edge finishes for fleece.

Avoid pressing fleece. Finger-press seams open or hold the iron above the surface and steam. Touching the iron to the fleece may leave a mark and heat can melt the fleece.

Ribbing serged to the seam line is an attractive finish for sleeve, hem and neckline edges.

Precut spandex trim strips are ideal for binding fleece edges, as the exposed raw edge sinks into the pile. To apply trim strips:

1. Trim the fleece edges evenly, if necessary.

2. With raw edges even, stitch the trim strip to the fleece using a narrow zigzag stitch as shown in Fig. 4.31.

Fig. 4.31
Stitch trim strip to fleece using narrow zigzag stitch.

3. Fold the trim strip over the edge, covering the stitching on the reverse side. Stitch in the ditch to secure the trim strip as shown in Fig. 4.32.

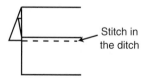

Stitch in the ditch

Fig. 4.32
Fold trim strip over edge, covering stitching on reverse side. Stitch in the ditch.

4. Cut the excess trim strip close to the stitching as shown in Fig. 4.33.

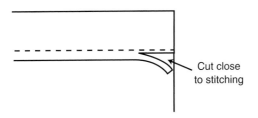

Fig. 4.33
Cut away excess trim strip close to stitching.

Because fleece is a stretch knit and stitches sink into it, zippers usually work better than buttonholes on fleece garments. See Closing Time on page 44 for zipper applications. If you do want to apply buttonholes to your knit garment, follow these steps:

1. For each buttonhole, apply water-soluble stabilizer to the right side and tear-away stabilizer to the wrong side of the fabric where the buttonhole will be stitched. Mark the buttonhole on the stabilizer. This helps to keep the stitches on top of the fabric.

2. To stitch the buttonhole, loosen the satin-stitch density so the fabric shows slightly between the stitches as shown in Fig. 4.34.

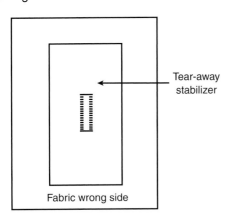

Fig. 4.34
Adjust satin-stitch density so fabric shows slightly between stitches.

Velvet

Luxurious velvet fabrics are beautiful to use for reversible double-layer sewing. However, due to its delicate nap and slippery nature, it can present challenges to even the most experienced sewers. Keep the following tips and techniques in mind to minimize frustration and ensure a successful sewing experience.

There are a couple of must-have tools available to make sewing with velvet more successful. A velvet V

sewing machine foot will enable you to stitch velvet without flattening the nap at the seam lines. A special velvet pressing cloth, such as a Velvaboard™, will prevent velvet nap from flattening during pressing.

Planning and Cutting
Fit any patterns before cutting the fabric. Making adjustments and removing stitches from velvet will leave marks.

Use a "with-nap" layout and pin pattern pieces to the velvet within the seam allowances.

Cut velvets that slide in a single layer. Less-slippery cotton velvets can be cut double layer.

Construction and Pressing
Use a new needle to begin your project.

Pin the seam allowances of the fabric layers together plentifully to prevent slipping.

Stitch in the nap direction. Avoid backstitching. Stitch with a short stitch length at the beginning and end of each seam instead as shown in Fig. 4.35.

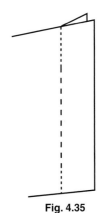

Fig. 4.35
Use a short stitch length at the beginning and end of each seam as shown.

Finish all seams, even those that won't show, to prevent raveling. Use sheer tricot tape to bind the seam allowances, or serge them.

To press cotton velvets, use a steam iron to press from the wrong side. To press other velvets, avoid pressing as much as possible and press lightly on the wrong side; do not let the iron rest on the fabric.

Embellishments
Velvet is fun to embellish by embossing with stamps or etching with Fiber Etch™ Fabric Remover. See Artistic Surface Treatments on page 54 to embellish your fabric with either of these techniques. ✄

Closing Time

Whether you decide to use double or single layers for your reversible sewing project, special considerations must be made for the closure to look attractive on both sides. Choose from the following techniques to select the one that best suits the fabric you're using and the look you want to achieve.

Buttonholes

Almost any buttonhole style can be used on reversible garments, but the main consideration is placement. Finish the garment edges before applying all but in-seam buttonholes. Practice stitching buttonholes on fabric scraps, making any necessary stitching adjustments until the buttonholes look as attractive on the back as the front.

Button Links

This versatile treatment is ideal for a variety of garment

styles and requires using purchased linked buttons or making your own. The latter affords you an unlimited range of button styles—any button with a shank can be used. The garment can be buttoned right over left or left over right when either side is worn on the outside.

1. Mark the buttonholes on each garment edge as shown in Fig. 5.01, making sure they will align exactly when the edges are overlapped.

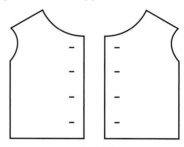

Fig. 5.01
Mark buttonholes on each garment edge, making sure they will align when edges are overlapped.

Special considerations must be made for the closure to look attractive on both sides.

2. Stitch the buttonholes and cut them open.

3. To make each button link, use heavy-duty thread to hand-sew the shanks together as shown in Fig. 5.02.

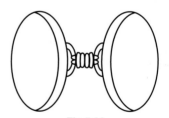

Fig 5.02
Use heavy-duty thread to hand-sew button shanks together to make linked buttons.

Double-Breasted

For this technique, it's necessary to use a pattern designed or adapted for a double-breasted front closure. See Garment Pattern Adjustments on page 8.

1. Mark and stitch buttonholes on each front edge.

2. Place the garment right side up on a flat surface and lap the right front over the left front. Mark the button placement on the left front. Sew the buttons in place as shown in Fig. 5.03.

Fig. 5.03
Lap right front over left. Mark button placement on left and sew buttons in place.

3. Reverse the garment and repeat to mark and add buttons to the left front as shown in Fig. 5.04.

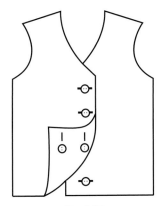

Fig. 5.04
Reverse garment. Mark button placement on left and sew in place.

In-Seam Buttonholes

In-seam buttonholes are suitable for a double-layer garment if the pattern was adjusted to meet at the center front and a band edge finish is planned. The buttonholes will be vertical. You can apply them to both garment fronts and use button links, or apply them only to the right front; the garment will button left over right when it's reversed.

1. Mark the buttonhole placements on the garment front right edge or both front edges as shown in Fig. 5.05.

2. Right sides facing, stitch the band to the front, stopping and backstitching at the buttonhole edges as shown in Fig. 5.06. Press the seam open.

3. Press under the seam allowances on the garment

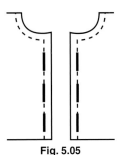

Fig. 5.05
Mark buttonhole placement on garment front right edge or both front edges.

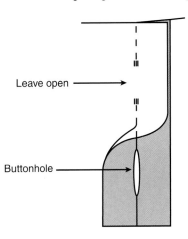

Fig. 5.06
Stitch band to garment front, stopping and backstitching at buttonhole edges.

reverse side and the remaining band edge. Slipstitch the edges together, leaving the seam open at each buttonhole as shown in Fig. 5.07.

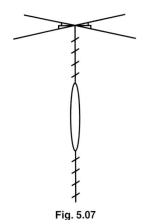

Fig. 5.07
Slipstitch edges together on reverse side leaving open at each buttonhole.

4. Slipstitch the layers together at the edges of each buttonhole.

5. Sew buttons to both sides of the left front band seam line to correspond with the buttonholes. Make button links if you applied buttonholes to both bands.

Traditional Placement

Traditional buttonholes stitched in the garment right front can be used for a reversible garment if you don't mind the garment buttoning left over right when it's reversed.

1. Mark and stitch buttonholes on the garment right front as usual.

2. Lap the right front over the left front and mark button placements. Reverse the garment and lap the left front over the right front to mark button placements.

3. Sew buttons to each side of the front as shown in Fig. 5.08.

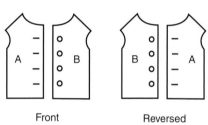

Front   Reversed

Fig. 5.08
Sew buttons to both sides of left front
to correspond with buttonholes.

Lacing

Lacing is an interesting closure for casual garments and accessories as well. Apply buttonholes or grommets and use ribbon or cord for the lacing. For garments, lacing can be used to close a front edge or as a decorative element on a side or sleeve seam.

For front closures, use a pattern adapted to meet in the center front. See Garment Pattern Adjustments on page 8. Finish the front edges and mark the buttonhole or grommet locations.

For side or sleeve seams, leave the seam open and finish the edges where you want to apply buttonholes or grommets for lacing. Mark the buttonhole or grommet locations as shown in Fig. 5.09.

Stitch a buttonhole at each mark or apply grommets.

Applying Grommets

Metal grommets in silver or gold tones are available in several sizes and must be applied with an applicator tool. They consist of a washer and a barrel with a flange as shown in Fig. 5.10.

Use them on double layers of fabrics ranging from lightweight cottons to heavyweight canvas and denim. Because of their weight, grommets usually are unsuitable for single-layer application.

1. Apply grommets to a doubled edge, reinforcing the wrong side of the fabric with an extra strip of fabric or twill tape.

2. Mark the grommet placement on the fabric. For small grommets, mark a dot at each placement; for large grommets, trace the grommet inside perimeter at each placement.

3. Use small, sharp scissors to make a hole at each dot or to cut an X inside each circle, then trim along the traced circle as shown in Fig. 5.11.

4. Follow the manufac-

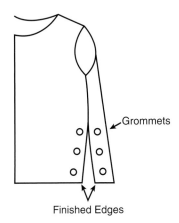

Grommets

Finished Edges

Fig. 5.09
Mark buttonhole or grommet location on
finished edges.

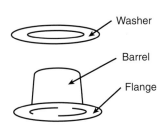

Washer

Barrel

Flange

Fig. 5.10
Each grommet consists of a washer and
a barrel with a flange.

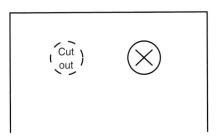

Cut
out

Fig. 5.11
Make a hole or cut an X in each marked
grommet circle and trim as shown.

turer's instructions and use the applicator to apply
the grommets.

Loops and Frogs

Loops and traditional buttons or frogs used with ball
buttons are attractive closures for many garment
styles, and can also be used as a decorative element
on pillows and other accessories.

Button loops are set into the edge seam and must
be used on double-layer garments assembled with
right sides facing as shown in Fig. 5.12. Frogs are
stitched to the surface with the loops extending over
the edge and can be used on any single- or double-

Fig. 5.12
Button loops are set in the edge seam
of double-layer garments assembled
with right sides facing.

Fig. 5.13
Frogs are stitched to garment surface
with loops extending over the edge.

layer garments as shown in Fig. 5.13.

For either closure on a garment, you will need to
adjust the right front only of an overlapping pattern to
a center closure. See Garment Pattern Adjustments
on page 8. Loops or frogs can be made of self-fabric
tubes or small tubular purchased trim, such as silky
rattail or leather cord, velvet tubing or other narrow,
flexible trim. Using either closure, garments will close
left over right when reversed. Apply buttons or balls to
both sides of the right front.

Making Loops

1. To determine the button loop size and spacing, on a
piece of paper draw a line ⅝" from the edge to represent the seam allowance. Draw a line within the seam
allowance, ¼" from the edge as shown in Fig. 5.14.
This will be the line for the loop ends and the outer-
most line will be the button position line.

2. Center the button on the position line, and wrap
cord around the button. Mark the cord ends at the line
to determine the loop length. Mark the paper above
and below the cord edges to determine the loop spacing as shown in Fig. 5.15

3. Using the determined measurements, cut cord
lengths and use self-adhesive double-sided basting

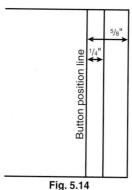

Fig. 5.14
Draw a line ⅝" from edge of paper and another ¼" as shown for button loop size and spacing.

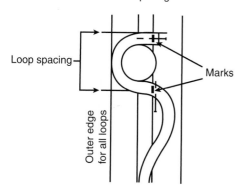

Fig. 5.15
Wrap cord around button on position line. Mark cord ends at the line to determine loop length. Mark above and below to determine spacing.

tape to adhere loops to the fabric seam allowance. Position the cut ends of the loops toward the edge.

4. With right sides facing, sew the remaining fabric layer in place, sandwiching the loops between the layers as shown in Fig 5.16.

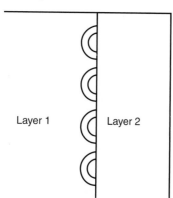

Layer 1   Layer 2

Fig. 5.16
Sandwich loops between fabric layers.

5. Trim and grade the seam allowances. Turn the layers right side out and press the seam. The loops will extend beyond the garment edge as shown in Fig. 5.17.

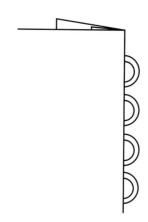

Fig. 5.17
When layers are turned right side out, loops will extend as shown.

6. Lap the right front with loops over the left front and mark button placements. Repeat for the reverse side, lapping the left front with loops over the right front. Sew buttons onto each side.

Frogs and Chinese Ball Buttons

Experiment with cording widths and practice making frogs and Chinese ball buttons until you achieve uniform results.

Chinese Ball Buttons

The cord diameter will affect the length required and the finished button size. To make each button:

1. Cut a 12"–16" length of cord. Pin one end to a piece of paper.

2. Make loops as shown in Fig. 5.18.

Fig. 5.18
Pin one end of cord to paper and make loops as shown.

3. Gradually tighten the loops to create a ball shape. Trim the ends of the cord and tack them flatly to the underside of the ball as shown in Fig. 5.19.

Finished button

Tack ends to
ball backside

Fig. 5.19
Gradually tighten loops to create ball
shape. Trim ends and tack to back of ball.

Frogs

Frogs are traditionally used in pairs with one attached to the ball button for decoration and the other attached to the opposite front for a closing loop. A frog can also be used individually as a closing loop for a ball button as shown in Fig. 5.20.

Fig. 5.20
Use frogs in pairs or use a single frog
with a ball button.

1. Draw the frog design on a piece of paper. For a clover design as shown, you can draw all loops the same size or one loop longer for the button loop. This will be your template for creating identical frogs.

2. Leaving a ¼" end and beginning at the center of the design, pin the cord to the paper, following the drawn design as shown. Conceal the ends on the wrong side of the frog as shown in Fig. 5.21.

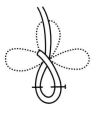  

Fig. 5.21
Starting at center, pin tubing to paper and follow design shown.
Conceal ends on wrong side of frog and hand-tack.

3. Using a needle and thread, hand-tack the cording intersections on the wrong side.

4. Remove the frog from the paper and turn it right side up. For a button decoration, slipstitch a ball button to a

loop. For a closure, place the frog on the garment with the button loop extending over the edge as shown in Fig. 5.22 and slipstitch it in place. Be sure to securely stitch the loop intersection because it is a point of stress.

Fig. 5.22
For a frog closure, place on garment
with loop extending over edge as shown.

Ties

Ties add interest as closures for garments and accessories and also serve a practical purpose for chair ties and window panels. Fabric ties are easy to make in matching or contrasting fabrics using one of the following techniques, and they're even easier if you use

handy tube-turning tools. Ribbon, bias tubing and other trims that are flexible and attractive on both sides are also good choices for ties. Use them for single- or double-layer projects.

1. For a garment front closure, adapt the pattern overlap to meet in the center front. See Garment Pattern Adjustments on page 8.

2. Decide the length and width of the tie, keeping it in proportion to the project.

3. To make each 1"-wide or wider tie, cut a fabric strip equal to the desired tie length, plus ⅞" for seam allowances, and twice the desired width, plus ½" for seam allowances.

Fold the strip in half lengthwise, right sides facing, and stitch the long edges and one short edge using a ¼" seam allowance as shown in Fig. 5.23. Turn the tie right side out and press the seam.

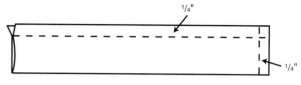

Fig. 5.23
Fold tie strip in half lengthwise, right sides facing. Stitch long edges and one short edge as shown.

4. To make a narrow tie, it's easier to make a folded and topstitched tie that doesn't need to be turned. Cut a fabric strip equal to the desired tie length, plus 1⅛" for seam allowances, and four times the desired strip width.

Press ½" under on one short end of the strip. Press the strip in half lengthwise, wrong sides facing. Fold the raw edges in to meet the center line and press. Topstitch close to each edge as shown in Fig. 5.24.

Fig. 5.24
For a very narrow tie, press strip in half lengthwise, wrong sides facing. Fold raw edges to meet at center line and topstitch close to both edges as shown.

5. To add ties to a double-layer project assembled with right sides facing, pin the ties to one fabric layer, aligning raw edges as shown in Fig. 5.25.

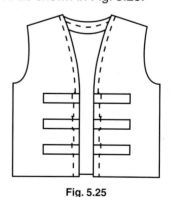

Fig. 5.25
For double-layer garment constructed right sides facing, pin ties to one layer, raw edges aligned.

Stitch the remaining fabric layer in place, sandwiching the tie ends. Turn right side out and press.

6. To add ties to double-layer projects assembled with wrong sides facing or single-layer projects, insert the tie end under the binding edge before stitching it in place as shown in Fig. 5.26.

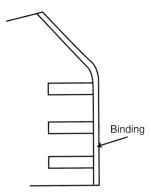

Fig. 5.26
For double-layer garment constructed wrong sides facing, or single-layer project, insert tie under binding before stitching.

Zippers

Reversible zippers are available in two slide styles: one with a flip-top slide that allows the pull to be placed on either side; the other style features a slide with a pull tab on each side. While your selection may be limited to separating sport zippers at the fabric store, with the exception of invisible zippers, you can special-order most zipper styles and weights with reversible sliders. Look for the order pad in the zipper section of the fabric store or ask a sales associate for assistance.

Patterns for garments with zipped front closures should be adapted to a center front closure if they aren't already. Apply zippers before finishing the neckline or hemline.

Double-Layer Zipper Applications

Use these applications for zippers to be applied between the fabric layers.

Enclosed Zipper

The zipper teeth are covered by the seam allowances in this application. It can be used for separating or non-separating zippers.

1. For non-separating zippers, the seam of each fabric layer should be stitched to the zipper opening.

2. On each fabric layer, press under the zipper opening

seam allowances. Baste ¼" from each fold to prevent the seam allowance from slipping.

3. Open the zipper and use self-adhesive double-sided basting tape to adhere the zipper halves between the seam allowances. Align the coil edges with the seam allowance folds on each garment side as shown in Fig. 5.27.

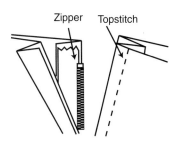

Fig. 5.27
Align zipper coils with seam allowance folds as shown.

4. Zip the zipper to make sure the seam allowance folds meet when the zipper is closed. Make any necessary adjustments.

5. Use a zipper foot and topstitch the zipper in place ¼" from the edges as shown in Fig. 5.28. Remove the basting threads.

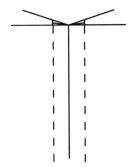

Fig. 5.28
Using zipper foot, topstitch zipper in place ¼" from edges.

Traditional Exposed Zipper

Use this application for a separating sport zipper, or any separating zipper where a casual look is desired. An exposed zipper with colorful plastic teeth can add a touch of fun to the front closure of a jacket or vest.

1. Follow the Enclosed Zipper instructions to press under and baste the seam allowances.

2. Use self-adhesive double-sided basting tape to adhere the zipper halves between the seam allowances. Align the edges of the seam allowances with the outer edge of the zipper teeth on each garment side as shown in Fig. 5.29.

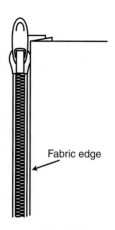

Fig. 5.29
Align edges of seam allowances with zipper teeth on each garment side.

3. Use a zipper foot and topstitch the zipper in place ¼" from the edges. Remove the basting threads.

Exposed Zipper With Decorative Seam Allowances

For non-fraying fabrics with a same or attractive wrong side, you can add a creative zipper application with exposed decorative seam allowances.

1. On each fabric layer, press the zipper opening seam allowances to the right side.

2. Slightly trim each seam allowance edge using a decorative blade.

3. Baste the seam allowances in place on the right side of each layer, ¼" from the edge.

4. Use self-adhesive double-sided basting tape to adhere the zipper halves between the seam allowances. Align the edges of the seam allowances with the outer edge of the zipper teeth on each garment side as shown in Fig. 5.30.

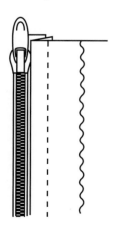

Fig. 5.30
Align edges of seam allowances with zipper teeth on each garment edge and stitch ¼" from zipper teeth.

Single-Layer Sewing Zipper Applications

You can use any of the zipper applications given for double-layer sewing to apply a zipper to a single layer of fabric, but you will need to disguise the zipper tape. Either cover the tape before the zipper is stitched in place or create a facing to cover the tape after stitching. You can also apply a Reverse Zipper that conceals the seam allowances using fleece-sewing expert Nancy Cornwell's clever technique.

Covering the Zipper Tape

To cover the zipper tape, you will need a ⅝"-wide length of ribbon or trim equal to the length of the zipper tape.

1. Cut the trim in half crosswise, then press each piece in half lengthwise.

2. Wrap the trim over each zipper tape and edge-stitch close to the zipper teeth as shown in Fig. 5.31.

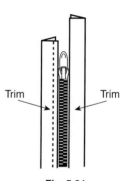

Trim   Trim

Fig. 5.31
Wrap zipper tape with decorative trim and edge-stitch close to zipper teeth.

3. Stitch the zipper in place, stitching again close to the edge of the covered tape, if necessary.

Creating Tape Facings

Cover the tape of a zipper that's already stitched in place with a creative trim facing. You will need ¾"-wide or wider trim in a length that's twice the zipper tape length. Add 6" to the required trim length for a non-separating zipper. Depending on the fabric, you can fuse or slipstitch the trim in place.

1. Apply the zipper using one of the techniques given for double-layer sewing.

2. Place the trim over the zipper tape length, covering the tape edges. Miter the lower corners as shown in Fig. 5.32 for a non-separating zipper.

3. Use fusible-web tape or permanent fabric glue to adhere the trim, or slipstitch it in place.

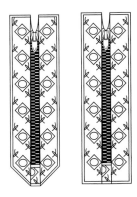

Fig 5.32
Place decorative trim over zipper that has been
stitched in place, mitering lower edges
as shown. Fuse or slipstitch in place.

Reverse Zipper

This application results in a finished edge on one side,
with the seam allowances and zipper tape hidden
under the trim on the reverse side. You will need ⅝"-
wide ribbon or trim equal to twice the zipper tape
length, plus a few extra inches.

1. Apply double-sided self-adhesive basting tape to
the outer edges of the zipper tape on the wrong side
of the zipper.

2. With wrong sides together, adhere the zipped zipper to the garment left front, aligning the tape and
front edges. Stitch the zipper in place using a ¼" seam
allowance as shown in Fig. 5.33.

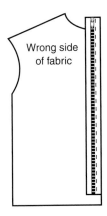

Fig. 5.33
Stitch wrong side of zipper to wrong
side of garment with ¼" seam allowance.

3. Wrong sides facing, adhere the remaining zipper

edge to the wrong side of the garment right front.
Unzip the zipper and stitch in place, using a ¼" seam
allowance.

4. Close the zipper and turn it to the right side. The
zipper should be right side up and the seam
allowances should be on the garment right side as
shown in Fig. 5.34.

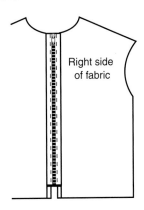

Fig. 5.34
Turn zipper to right side as shown.

5. Leaving ½" of trim extending beyond the garment
lower edge, use basting tape to adhere ribbon to the
zipper tape ⅛" from the teeth. Edge-stitch along the
edge closest to the teeth as shown in Fig. 5.35.

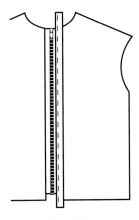

Fig. 5.35
Edge-stitch decorative trim over zipper tape.

6. Apply basting tape to the wrong side of the
unstitched ribbon edge and adhere it to the front.
Edge-stitch the remaining ribbon edge in place.

7. Repeat to cover the remaining zipper tape with ribbon.

8. Finish the neckline and hem edges as desired. ✄

Special Tips & Techniques

Matching Prints & Plaids

It looks attractive and professional to match prints and plaids at the seam line on any sewing project, but it's especially important on large projects such as window panels or duvet covers, where a wide area will be viewed at once.

A good general rule is to plan on purchasing one extra fabric repeat to ensure enough yardage. Be sure to match the patterns before cutting out any pieces from the fabric.

Always match the seam lines, not the cutting lines.

Be sure to match the patterns before cutting out any pieces from the fabric.

Garments and Projects Cut From Patterns

1. Position a main pattern piece on the fabric right side. Make sure the print or plaid falls on the piece in a pleasing manner. Cut out the piece.

2. Press under the seam allowance on the cut piece, then use it as a guide when cutting adjacent pieces, making certain the prints will match at the seam line.

3. To ensure exact stitching, apply basting tape to the pressed-under seam allowances. Adhere the seam allowance to the corresponding edge, matching the print or plaid as shown in Fig. 6.01.

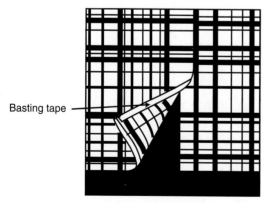

Basting tape

Fig. 6.01
Apply basting tape to ensure an exact match of print or plaid.

4. Stitch the seam from the garment wrong side, using the crease line as a stitching guide.

Measured Panels

1. For large panels, such as those used for window treatments or duvet covers, use a large right-angle or a T-square to mark a straight line across the fabric edge from selvage to selvage, making sure it is perpendicular to the selvage edge. Cut along the marked line to create the panel lower edge. Measure the desired distance and repeat to cut the panel upper edge.

2. To cut the adjacent panel, place the cut panel and the yardage with right sides together and the cut panel on top.

3. Fold back the upper panel selvage and adjust the placement until the print or plaid matches at the seam line as shown in Fig. 6.02.

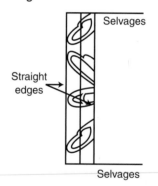

Selvages

Straight edges

Selvages

Fig. 6.02
With fabric panels facing, fold back upper panel selvage and adjust until panels match.

4. Pin or use basting tape to secure the edges. Baste the seam line, check the match, then cut the lower panel upper and lower edges.

5. Stitch the final seam.

Artistic Surface Treatments

Add an extra touch of creativity to your reversible sewing when you create your own one-of-a-kind fabrics with etching, embossing, stamping and stenciling. While stenciling is sometimes easier to position on a finished fabric panel, the rest of these treatments are best applied to the fabric before it's cut and sewn.

Fabric Etching

Thanks to the wonders of a product called Fiber Etch™ Fiber Remover, you can create burnout and cutwork designs on fabric. Most fabrics, except velvet, will appear the same on both sides and can be used as a single layer or with another layer that will show through the burned-out areas.

Fabric Selection

Fiber Etch dissolves fabrics made of cellulose (plant) fibers, such as cotton, linen, rayon, rayon satin, Tencel™ and ramie. Cutwork designs are achieved when the chemical is applied to fabric with a 100% cellulose fiber content.

Burnout and other etched effects result when the chemical is applied to fabrics with blends of cellulose and wool, silk or synthetic fibers; only the cellulose pile or threads are removed, leaving other fibers intact. Fabrics with a high cellulose fiber content will have more fibers removed than fabrics with a low cellulose fiber content.

To create a burnout look on velvet, use only velvet that has rayon pile and silk backing; the pile will be dissolved, leaving the backing intact.

Read the fabric bolt label and always test fabrics first, as the results will also vary with the fabric weave.

Design Planning and Etching

Create a stencil and etch the design as follows. See Velvet Tips at the end for special velvet instructions.

1. The first step is to decide on a design and create a freezer-paper stencil. Freezer paper adheres securely when ironed onto the fabric, preventing the Fiber Etch gel from seeping under the edges.

Draw the design to be etched on the unwaxed side of the freezer-paper. Cut out the areas to be etched. You can also cut out straight strips of freezer paper to create borders.

2. Press the fabric flat.

3. Position the design and border stencils shiny side down on the fabric and use medium heat and pressure to iron them in place; too much heat may result in

Add an extra touch of creativity to your reversible sewing when you create your own one-of-a-kind fabrics with etching, embossing, stamping and stenciling.

a permanent bond. Lightly iron the wrong side. Be sure all edges are securely adhered to the fabric.

Pin the fabric, stencil side up, to a paper-covered work surface. Squeeze a small amount of Fiber Etch gel into a small container. Dip a synthetic paintbrush into the gel and apply an even layer to the open stencil areas. Unpin the fabric and place it on dry newspaper. Use tissues or a small terry cloth towel to blot with pressure any residual—or shiny—areas of gel on the fabric or stencil; if left unblotted, these areas could burn holes into the fabric when activated. Place fabric on a dry surface and let it air dry. A hair dryer will speed up drying, especially in areas with small details. Remove the stencil.

4. To activate the gel, place the fabric and a small dry towel in the dryer and dry at a low temperature for 30 minutes. The treated areas

should be stiff, and the fibers should break away when the fabric is folded on the cross grain. Continue drying if any areas aren't completely activated, being careful not to let the treated areas turn brown. If the areas haven't been activated after an hour, remove the fabric from the dryer and iron it with low heat, using a press cloth and keeping the iron moving at all times until all areas are activated.

5. Rinse the fabric under warm running water, rubbing the design gently in a circular motion with a small terry cloth towel until the cellulose fibers are removed. For easy rinsing, cover a baking sheet with terry cloth, place the fabric on the sheet and hold it at an angle under the running water.

6. Let the fabric air dry and iron while damp, but not wet.

Velvet Tips

Consider these tips to successfully etch silk/rayon velvet:

• The silk backing is very delicate; be careful not to let it overheat or leave the Fiber Etch on longer than necessary.

• Check the velvet every few minutes after putting it in the dryer. The pile will be stiff and easily scratch away when it's ready.

• Rub gently as you rinse the velvet under running water.

• Wash the etched velvet gently with liquid soap and roll it in a towel to absorb the excess moisture. Tumble dry.

Embossing Velvet

Embossing velvet is another technique that's fun for creating your own custom-design fabric.

Use silk, rayon or rayon/acetate velvet for the best results. Nylon and polyester velvets won't emboss successfully.

Choose a rubber stamp with a large, bold design. Avoid intricate designs and details.

Do not press your embossed velvet or projects with steam or the embossing will disappear.

Emboss the velvet as follows:

1. Place the embossing stamp right side up on a heat-resistant surface.

2. Lightly mist the wrong side of the velvet with water.

3. Position the fabric right side down on top of the

stamp. Use a medium-hot dry iron and press it directly on top of the fabric and stamp as shown in Fig. 6.03.

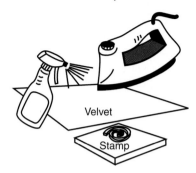

Fig. 6.03
Place the right side of velvet over embossing stamp and mist wrong side with water; press with medium-hot dry iron.

4. Hold the iron in place for 20 to 30 seconds, then lift it straight up, being careful not to slide it. Let the impression cool.

5. Repeat to create multiple embossed impressions.

Stamping

You can stamp almost any fabric, but natural-fiber fabrics like cotton, linen, or silk usually accept and retain the paint or ink colors the best. Suede, faux suede and velvet also are wonderful surfaces for stamping.

Stamps

Rubber, foam and clear polymer stamps can all be used. Clear stamps are especially designed for fabric and make it easy to see the placement of your design.

To select a stamp, consider the fabric texture as well as the look you want to achieve. A stamp with a large design area works well on textured or smooth fabrics, but a stamp with a detailed design is best used on a smooth surface. Textured fabrics often yield a more primitive, but interesting image.

Paints and Inks

Paints and inks specifically formulated for textiles will provide good coverage without stiffening the fabric, and are permanent after heat setting.

Fabric paints are thicker than inks and colors of the same brand can be mixed together to create new colors. The opacity and thickness of the paint varies between brands. Thicker paints will adhere the best to the stamps. Use a fabric paint roller to apply paint to the stamp.

Fabric inks are used with ink pads. They are available in pre-inked pads as well as bottled inks to be used with blank ink pads.

Stamping the Design

1. Wash and dry washable fabrics to remove the sizing.

2. Place the fabric on a paper-covered, smooth, hard surface to stamp.

3. To stamp with paint, pour fabric paint into the paint roller tray and roll the roller through the paint until it's evenly distributed. Scrape off any excess paint on the tray edge. Roll the paint thinly and evenly over the stamp surface, making sure excess paint isn't in the crevices or on the edges. Firmly press the stamp onto the fabric and lift up without sliding the stamp.

4. To stamp with ink, press the stamp onto the ink pad, then press it onto the fabric. Lift up without sliding the stamp.

5. Let the stamped design dry for 24–48 hours. Follow the paint or ink manufacturer's instructions to heat-set.

Stenciling

Stenciling is a great way to accent hemlines and the edges of home decor accessories like tablecloths, sheets and pillowcases. You'll need a pre-cut stencil, temporary stencil adhesive spray, stencil paint crèmes and stencil brushes.

1. Wash and dry washable fabrics. Press to remove any wrinkles.

2. Follow the manufacturer's instructions to spray the back of the stencil with adhesive and position it on the fabric.

3. Use a paper towel to remove the coating that forms on top of the stencil crème.

4. Dab the stencil brush into the paint, then onto a paper towel to remove the excess paint.

5. Hold the brush upright and use a circular motion to apply the paint to the stencil openings, working from the outside toward the center.

6. Follow the paint manufacturer's instructions for drying time and heat setting.

Technique Tricks

Sometimes the little things make a big difference, and that's what this section of the book is all about. Whether it's a technique to save your time or sanity, add a professional finishing touch, or just give you an idea, these little tricks and projects are sure to add to your reversible-sewing pleasure.

Handbag and Tote Tips

Handbags and totes are great reversible sewing projects. They require a minimum of fabric, are easy to make and are great for gift giving. Here are two quick-

finish assembly techniques guaranteed to have you mass-producing totes of all shapes and sizes.

Fold-Over Upper Edge

This technique results in a bag with a plain edge on one side and a banded upper edge on the reverse side.

1. Cut two panels in the width and height desired for the inner bag. For the outer bag, cut two panels equal in width to the inner panels, adding 1½" to the height.

2. Sew each set of panels together with right sides facing. Press the seams open. Turn the outer bag right side out.

3. Wrong sides facing, place the inner bag inside the outer bag, aligning the side seams.

4. Press the outer bag raw edge under ½", then press it under 1", overlapping the inner bag as shown in Fig. 6.04.

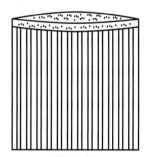

Fig. 6.04
Press raw edge of outer bag under ½"
and then again 1", overlapping the inner
bag as shown.

5. Pin, then topstitch the band in place along the lower edge and again ¼" from the upper edge.

6. Cut or make handles, turning the ends under. Stitch to each side of the bag as shown in Fig. 6.05.

Fig. 6.05
Stitch handles to each side of bag as shown.

Easy-Finish Upper Edge

This technique results in a bag with finished seam with handles on the upper side. The trick is in the turning.

1. Cut two panels in the width and height desired for the inner bag and two in the same measurements for the outer bag.

2. Sew each set of panels together with right sides facing, leaving a 3" opening in the lower edge seam of the inner bag. Press the seams open.

3. Turn the outer bag right side out. Make or cut two handles. Center and pin each handle to the right side of an outer bag panel, aligning the handle ends with the upper edge as shown in Fig. 6.06.

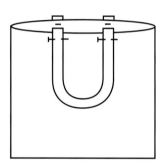

Fig. 6.06
Center and pin handles to right side
of outer bag, aligning raw edges.

4. Insert the outer bag into the inner bag with right sides facing and side seams and upper edges aligned. The handle ends should be sandwiched between the layers. Stitch the upper edges of the bags together as shown in Fig. 6.07.

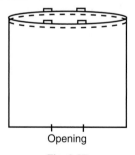

Opening

Fig. 6.07
Stitch the upper edges of the
inner and outer bags together.

5. Pull the outer bag through the lower edge opening of the inner bag, turning both bags right side out as shown in Fig. 6.08.

6. Slipstitch the opening closed. Insert the inner bag into the outer bag and press the upper edge seam. Topstitch close to the edge.

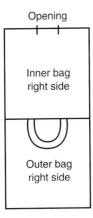

Fig. 6.08
Pull outer bag through opening in inner bag, turning both right side out.

Perfect Pillow Corners

If you've ever made a cover for a pillow form and ended up with floppy corners that looked like rabbit ears, then this cutting technique is for you. By tapering the edges to the corner, you're assured of perfect corners on square or rectangular covers.

1. Cut two pillow panels in the desired measurements.

2. Fold one panel into fourths, right sides facing, and pin the edges to secure.

3. Mark the distance halfway between the corner and the edge on two raw edges. Make another mark ½" from the corner and draw a line to connect the three marks as shown in Fig. 6.09.

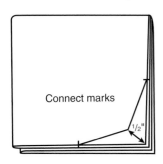

Fig. 6.09
Fold panel in quarters and mark center points on 2 edges as shown. Mark ½" in from the raw-edge corners and connect to side marks. Cut on marked lines through all layers.

4. Cut on the marked lines through all layers.

5. Open the trimmed panel and use it as a guide to shape the second panel.

6. Sew the panels right sides together, inserting any desired trims in the seams as instructed on page 15, and leaving an opening for turning.

7. Turn the panels right side out and slipstitch the opening closed.

Window Treatments

There are a number of creative ways to finish the upper edge of a window treatment. From rod pockets, decorative tabs and grommets to treatments that button onto or drape over a fabric-covered rod, it's easy to add the perfect finishing touch to your reversible valance or drapery panels.

Drapery rods vary in size and include round and flat metal or wood rods. Padded and covered PVC pipe with finials also makes an attractive and eye-catching treatment for tab-top panels or swags that drape over the rod. Always plan the hanging treatment and choose the drapery rod before you cut the panels from fabric.

Rod Pockets

The basic rod pocket with a header is a functional and easy-to-sew upper edge finish for valances and curtain or drapery panels. It usually looks best on treatments that will be gathered on the rod rather than lying flat. Rod pockets can be sewn with or without a header above the pocket.

The rod pocket depth depends on the size of the drapery rod, plus an allowance for the fabric to glide smoothly over the rod. Generally, increase the allowance with the size of the rod. To determine the depth, add 1"–2" to the diameter of a round rod, or ½"–1" to the width of a flat rod.

The header depth depends on both the style and size of the window treatment. A smaller 1"–2" header is sufficient on most valances and standard panels, but you can make them up to 4" for large windows or very gathered country curtains.

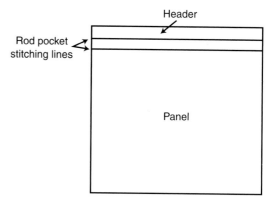

Fig. 6.10
Mark upper and lower stitching lines for rod pocket.

To sew a basic rod pocket:

1. On the right side of each panel upper edge, use chalk to mark the header depth for the rod pocket upper stitching line. Draw a parallel line to mark the rod pocket lower stitching line as shown in Fig. 6.10.

2. For deep headers or headers on soft fabrics, fuse a strip of interfacing to the header wrong side.

3. Sew the panels together, finishing the edges as desired and leaving the rod pocket edges open.

4. With the panels right side out, turn under and press the rod pocket raw edges.

5. Pin the panels together on each side of the rod pocket markings, making sure the panels are straight and flat.

6. Stitch along the marked rod pocket lines.

Tab Tops

Tabs are a fun and creative hanging technique and are best used on window treatments that are flat or 1½–2 times the window width; the tab effect will be lost on very

gathered edges. You can design matching fabric tabs in the width or shape of your choice, or you can use wide ribbon or cording.

When planning the cut panel length, plan to hang them so the panel upper edge will be at least 2" above the window frame. This will prevent light from showing between the panel and window upper edges.

Keep the size of the tabs in proportion to the panel size and style. To determine the length to cut the tabs, wrap a scrap of fabric around the rod and pin it to the panel. Adjust the fit until the tab slides easily. Measure the tab length and add 1¼" for seam allowances as shown in Fig. 6.11.

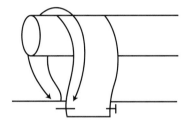

Fig. 6.11
Measure tab length and add 1¼" for seam allowance.

Tab spacing is a matter of choice and depends on the look you want to achieve. For a drooping or draping effect, space the tabs farther apart. If you'd like a straight edge, space them closer together.

To make and attach basic tabs:

1. For each tab, cut two fabric strips in the desired width, plus 1¼" for seam allowances and the deter- mined length.

2. Stitch the long edges together. Trim the seam allow- ances and turn the tabs right side out. Press them flat.

3. Fold the tab in half and baste the raw edges togeth- er to prevent shifting when sewing them to the panel as shown in Fig. 6.12.

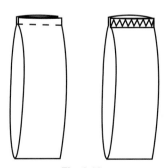

Fig. 6.12
Stitch or serge tab ends together to prevent shifting during application.

4. Evenly space the tabs on the right side of one panel, aligning raw edges. Begin and end ¾" from the panel edges. Baste the tab edges in place as shown in Fig. 6.13.

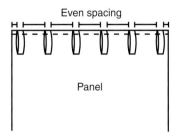

Fig. 6.13
Space tabs evenly across right side of one panel, aligning raw edges.

5. Right sides together, stitch the remaining panel in place, leaving a 6" opening in one side seam as shown in Fig. 6.14.

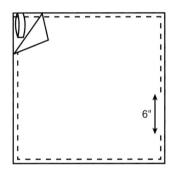

Fig. 6.14
Stitch remaining panel in place, leaving a 6" opening in one side for turning.

6. Clip the corners diagonally and trim the seam allowances to ¼". Turn the panels right side out and press, pressing under the seam allowances on the opening. Slipstitch the opening closed.

7. Topstitch along the upper edge of the panel, if desired.

Buttonholes and Grommets
Buttonholes and grommets add a casual, attractive touch to window treatments and offer a variety of cre- ative hanging options. Completely finish the valance or panels to be hung and follow the instructions in Closing Time on page 44 to apply grommets or stitch buttonholes in the upper edge.

Apply evenly spaced buttonholes or grommets along the upper edge. Weave a narrow, round curtain rod through the openings as shown in Fig. 6.15.

Apply buttonholes to the panel upper edge. Cover a flat drapery rod with fabric. Sew buttons onto the rod to correspond with the panel buttonholes, then button

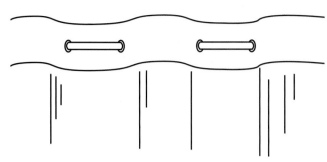

Fig. 6.15
Weave narrow rod through openings as shown.

the panel onto the rod as shown in Fig. 6.16.

Screw small knobs or hooks into the upper edge of a window frame as shown in Fig. 6.17. Stitch button-holes or apply grommets to the panel upper edge, then attach to the knobs or hooks.

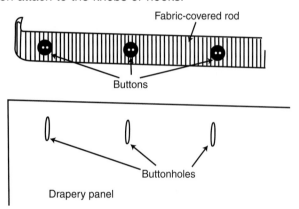

Fig. 6.16
Button drapery panel onto fabric-covered rod.

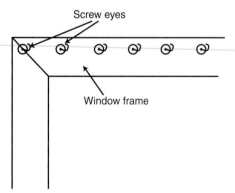

Fig. 6.17
Screw small knobs or hooks
into window frame as shown.

Foundation-Pieced Patchwork

Do you have a piece of velvet that's too small to make into a project, but too luscious to toss? How about a beautiful snippet of embroidered satin? Foundation-pieced patchwork is a great way to showcase small pieces of great fabrics and trim scraps left over from

other projects. Reminiscent of Victorian crazy quilting, this technique offers a fun and easy way to create patchwork for garments and accessories, including vests, table runners and pillow panels. Straight lines are easiest to sew and it's best to use a pattern with-out construction details, such as darts or gathers.

You have the choice of piecing the patchwork on one or both sides of the foundation fabric. On single-sided patchwork, the reverse side will feature the stitching used to sew the patchwork pieces in place. On double-sided patchwork, both sides of the project will feature an identical pieced design, although the fabrics can be different on each side. For either technique, preshrink and press washable fabrics before beginning.

Single-Sided Patchwork

Choose a sturdy fabric, such as broadcloth, for the foundation. For the patchwork, select an attractive assortment of fabrics in similar weights. Cotton, satin, wool and velvet fabrics all are beautiful when pieced in this manner. Consider incorporating lace, ribbon and other trim scraps into the seam lines as you stitch. Use a ¼" seam allowance for piecing the patchwork.

Mark the patchwork design on the foundation fabric and use the lines as a guide to cut and piece the patchwork, or use the following steps to create crazy quilting.

1. Cut the pattern piece or pieces from the founda-tion fabric.

2. From the patchwork fabric, cut an irregular shape with straight edges. Center this piece right side up on the foundation fabric wrong side and topstitch the edges in place.

3. From a different patchwork fabric, cut another irreg-ular shape. With right sides together and the raw edges on one side of each piece aligned, pin it to the stitched piece. Stitch the aligned edges together, sewing through all layers as shown in Fig. 6.18.

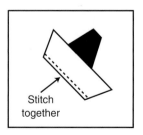

Fig. 6.18
Right sides together, stitch fabric
pieces together along one edge
as shown.

4. Turn the second piece right side up and press it flat. Trim the unsewn raw edges of the adjoining pieces to form straight lines.

5. From a third fabric, cut another patchwork piece with one edge long enough to cover one edge of the two stitched fabrics. Pin, then stitch it right sides facing to the first two fabrics as shown in Fig. 6.19.

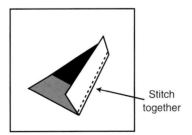

Stitch together

Fig. 6.19
Right sides facing, place another fabric piece along edges of first two and stitch as shown.

6. Turn the third piece right side up and press it flat. Trim the edges even with the first two pieces, forming straight lines.

7. Repeat to cover the entire foundation piece, including the edges, with patchwork. Work from the center out and add any trims to the seams as you sew.

8. If desired, embellish the finished seams with decorative stitching. Traditional Victorian crazy-quilting stitches include herringbone, feather, star and cross stitches as shown in the photo.

9. Trim the patchwork even with the foundation edges.

10. Check the finished piece with the original pattern, trimming the pieced edges if necessary.

11. Assemble the project and bind the edges, referring to Reversible Single-Layer Sewing on page 31.

Double-Layer Foundation Piecing

Perfect for creating double-duty pieced projects, this technique requires advance planning of the finished patchwork. The pieces on each side of the foundation will be the same and sewn to the foundation fabric simultaneously. Use broadcloth, muslin or silk organza for the foundation fabric. Cotton, wool and other nonslippery fabrics are easiest to use for the patchwork. Use a ¼" seam allowance for all piecing.

1. Cut the pattern piece or pieces from the foundation fabric.

2. Draw the piecing pattern design on one side of the foundation fabric, then retrace the lines on the other side. Label each segment of the design as shown in Fig. 6.20. If necessary, hold the fabric to a light box or window to see the lines and ensure accuracy as you draw.

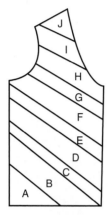

Fig. 6.20
Draw piecing pattern on one side of
foundation fabric and then on the other.
Label as shown.

3. To make templates for the patchwork, trace each section of the piecing pattern onto pattern tracing cloth, adding ¼" seam allowances to all drawn lines. Label each piece as shown in Fig. 6.21.

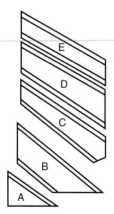

Fig. 6.21
Trace each section of the piecing pattern
onto pattern tracing material, adding ¼"
seam allowances to all drawn lines. Label
each piece as shown.

4. For each side of the project, use the templates to cut the patchwork pieces from fabric. Label each piece to correspond with the pattern.

5. Begin at the lower edge of the foundation piece and pin a corresponding patchwork piece, right side up, to each side of the foundation. Baste in place along the marked seam line and all edges as shown in Fig. 6.22.

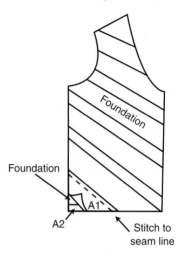

Fig. 6.22
Beginning at lower edge of foundation,
pin a corresponding patchwork piece,
right side up, to each side of foundation.
Baste in place on seam lines.

6. On each side of the foundation piece, pin the next pair of patches right side down over the first piece, aligning upper edges. Stitch the upper edges together along the seam line as shown in Fig. 6.23.

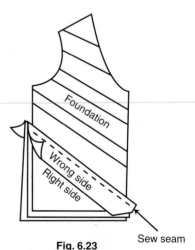

Fig. 6.23
On each side of foundation, pin next
patches right side down over first,
aligning upper edges. Stitch along
seam line as shown.

7. Turn the second pair of pieces right side up and press flat.

8. Repeat to add the remaining patchwork pieces in pairs, working from the lower edge up as shown in Fig. 6.24.

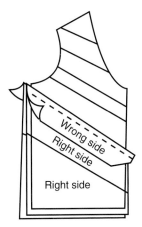

Fig. 6.24
Continue adding each pair of patches,
front and back, working from lower edge
to upper edge.

9. Embellish the seam lines with decorative stitching, if desired.

10. Check the finished piece with the original pattern, trimming the pieced edges if necessary.

11. Assemble the project and bind the edges, referring to Reversible Single-Layer Sewing on page 31.

Reverse Outline Stitching

Reverse outline stitching can be used on almost any project that's made with two layers of fabric and a layer of batting in between, or with a lofty fabric such as chenille or fleece for one side and a print fabric for the reverse.

For one fabric, use a print that's large or has distinguishable motifs that are suitable for stitching around.

For the reverse side, use a solid color or mini-print fabric, fleece or chenille.

1. Follow the instructions for Reversible Double-Layer Sewing on page 11 to construct the project, adding batting between the layers if you're not using a lofty fabric. If you want to add reverse outline stitching to the sleeves on a jacket, add it before sewing the sleeve seam.

2. Stitch with the print fabric right side up. Lower the feed dogs on your sewing machine. Use No. 8 pearl cotton in the bobbin and No. 30 thread in the needle. Practice stitching on layered fabric scraps before beginning.

3. Stitch along the fabric print outline with the No. 30 thread. The pearl cotton will create outline stitching on the reverse side. ✂

Patterns

Lamp Cover & Table Mat

By Chris Malone

*Custom fabrics lend a decorator look to even the thriftiest lamp you can buy.
And when you make these projects reversible, you double your time and your money!*

Project Specifications

Skill Level: Beginner

Lamp Size: Any size (Model lamp base is 8½" in height. Shade is 4" x 7" x 10".)

Table Mat Size: 24" x 24"

Note: *If lamp is larger than model, adjust fabric yardage accordingly.*

Materials

For Fabric Lamp Base Cover & Shade

- Lamp with shade
- ¾–1 yard of 2 home decor fabrics—one green check and one coordinating floral
- 4 yards of ecru piping
- 28" ecru twisted cotton cord with tassels
- 1⅓ yards of ⅜"-wide green grosgrain ribbon
- All-purpose sewing threads to match fabrics
- Newsprint or large sheet of pattern paper
- String
- Thumbtack
- Marker
- Seam sealant (optional)
- Zipper foot
- Basic sewing supplies and tools

For Table Mat

- 31" x 31" square of green check home decor fabric
- 24" x 24" square of coordinating floral home décor fabric
- All-purpose sewing threads to match fabrics
- Basic sewing supplies and tools

Instructions

Project Note: *All seams are ½" unless otherwise noted.*

Fabric Lamp Base Cover

Step 1. Measure lamp base from top edge of neck on one side, down and under lamp and up to top edge on other side as shown in Fig. 1. Add 7" to this measurement for total pattern size.

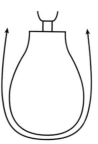

Fig. 1
Measure lamp base as shown and add 7" for pattern size.

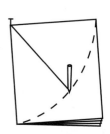

Fig. 2
Swing marker from one edge of paper to the other as shown.

Step 2. Fold large sheet of newsprint or pattern paper in half two times. Tie one end of string around marker. From the marker, measure one-half the distance totaled in Step 1 and insert thumbtack through string. Insert thumbtack at folded corner of paper. Swing marker from one edge of paper to the other as shown in Fig. 2. Unfold paper. The circle created is the pattern for the lamp cover.

Step 3. Cut a circle from each fabric using circle pattern.

Step 4. Pin ecru piping to right side of one fabric circle, raw edges aligned. With zipper foot, baste piping close to cord. Begin stitching 1" from end of piping. Stop stitching a few inches from starting point and open piping. Trim cord to butt up against other end of cord. Fold raw end of bias strip under and wrap it around the two cord ends. Finish stitching.

Step 5. Pin two fabric circles together, right sides facing, and sew all around, leaving a 5" opening for turning. Grade seam by trimming piping strip close to the seam. Clip curves and turn right side out. Close opening with hand stitches.

Step 6. Place lamp base on center of fabric circle and mark the spot where the lamp cord extends from the base of lamp. Cut a slit through both layers of fabric large enough for plug to fit through. Finish slit as a buttonhole by hand or machine or apply seam sealant and allow to dry before pulling cord through opening. **Note:** *If making a machine buttonhole, cut slit after buttonhole is sewn.*

Step 7. Bring edges of fabric up around neck of lamp. Wrap tasseled cord around fabric; knot cord as shown in photo.

Lamp Shade

Step 1. Place seam of lamp shade ½" from edge of newsprint or pattern paper. Carefully roll the shade across the paper, marking the paper along the bottom edge of the shade as it moves. Stop when you return to the seam. Repeat to mark the top of the shade. Add ½" seam allowance all around and cut out the pattern.

Step 2. Cut one shade cover from each fabric using paper pattern.

Step 3. Pin ecru piping to right side of one fabric along lower edge. Open piping at both ends and trim ¾" from the end of the cord. Pull the ends up into the seam allowance so piping recedes into the seam at both ends. Repeat at the top edge of the shade cover. With zipper foot, baste piping in place.

Step 4. Cut green grosgrain ribbon into six 8" lengths. Pin ends of three ribbons down each straight edge of

one shade cover. Position one at top and bottom, just outside of seam line, and one in the middle. Align cut edges of ribbon with raw edges of fabric. Machine-stitch down straight edges to catch ribbon ends and to stabilize the fabric to prevent stretching.

Step 5. Pin two fabric shade covers together, right sides facing. Sew top and bottom seams. Grade seam allowance as in Step 5, Fabric Lamp Base Cover. Turn right side out through one side opening; press.

Step 6. Fold in seam allowances on straight edges; press and slipstitch to close openings.

Step 7. Wrap cover around shade and tie ribbons in bows as shown in photo.

Table Mat

Step 1. Press under ½" hem on all sides of green check square.

Step 2. Place green check square on flat work surface, wrong side up. Center floral square on top, right side up. Pin or baste securely.

Step 3. Press green check fabric up and over the edges of the floral fabric. Fold and miter corners as shown in Fig. 3. Trim excess fabric from corner ½" from diagonal fold. Slipstitch folded edges of miter together. Repeat at each corner.

Fig. 3
Fold and miter corners as shown.

Step 4. Topstitch inner edge of green check fabric to finish. ✄

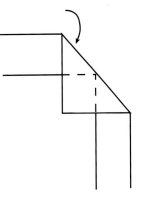

Classic Elegance Valance

By Marian Shenk

The two fabrics used for this valance are pleasingly coordinated,
but they could be very different for a major change in decor.

Project Specifications

Skill Level: Beginner
Valance Size: Approximately 53½" x 13½"

Materials

- ¾ yard 54"-wide floral decorator fabric
- 1 yard 54"-wide blue solid moiré
- 2½ yards of 1½"-wide blue tassel fringe
- Newsprint or large pieces of pattern paper
- All-purpose threads to match fabrics
- Basic sewing supplies and tools

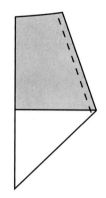

Fig. 2
Sew seam and short side as shown.

Instructions

Step 1. Cut tabs as instructed on pattern. Fold tab in half lengthwise, right sides together, and stitch with a ¼" seam across bottom edge. Turn right side out, placing seam at center fold and folding on fold lines, creating a point as shown in Fig. 1.

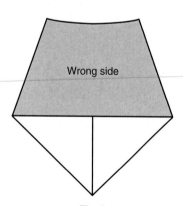

Fig. 1
Fold as shown to create point.

Step 2. Fold in half again lengthwise, right sides together. Sew with ¼" seam on short side as shown in Fig. 2.

Step 3. Turn right side out and press to make tab as shown in Fig. 3. Repeat for five tabs.

Step 4. From newsprint or pattern paper cut and piece a rectangle 54" x 14½". Fold in half, bringing short ends together. Place one end of scallop pattern at fold.

Trace curve and repeat three times as shown in Fig. 4, ending last repeat 1½" from edge. Extend top edge of last repeat to outer edge of paper, again referring to Fig. 4. Cut out paper pattern. Cut one floral and one blue solid valance piece.

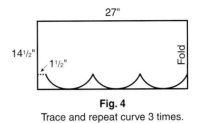

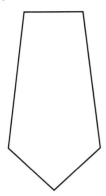

Fig. 3
Turn right side out and press
to make tab as shown.

Step 5. Place two fabric layers together, right sides facing. With ¼" seam allowance, sew layers together down sides and around scallops. Clip seams, turn right side out and press.

Step 6. Place five tabs on valance with points between each scallop as shown in Fig. 5. Baste in place.

Step 7. From newsprint or pattern paper cut and piece a rectangle 54" x 10½". Fold in half, bringing short ends together. Place one end of scallop pattern at fold. Trace curve and repeat three times as shown in

Fig. 4
Trace and repeat curve 3 times.

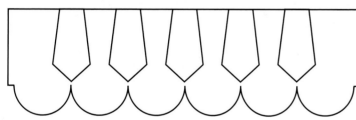

Fig. 5
Place tabs as shown.

Classic Elegance Valance
Scallop Pattern

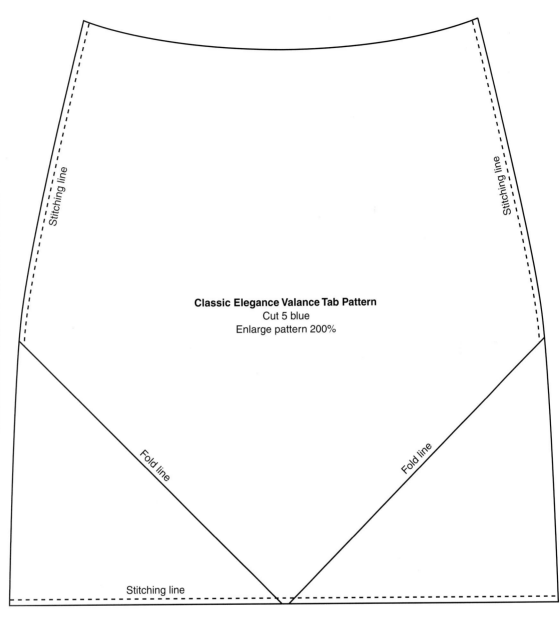

Classic Elegance Valance Tab Pattern
Cut 5 blue
Enlarge pattern 200%

Stitching line

Stitching line

Fold line

Fold line

Stitching line

Fig. 6, ending last repeat 1½" from edge. Extend top edge of last repeat diagonally up to outer edge of paper, again referring to Fig. 6. Cut out paper pattern. Cut one valance piece from floral fabric.

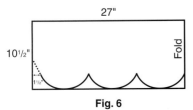

27"

10½"

Fold

1½"

Fig. 6
Trace and repeat curve 3 times.

Step 8. Align backside of seam allowance of 1½"-wide blue tassel fringe with right side of scalloped raw edge of valance cut in Step 7. Edge-stitch in place. Turn seam allowance to back of valance and topstitch ⅜" from edge on right side to secure fringe.

Step 9. Place right sides of two floral sections together and stitch across top. Fold fringed section over so that it is on top of blue solid valance; press.

Step 10. Mark 3" from top and stitch across to make casing for 2½" rod. Sew along side edges from casing down to fringe to hold layers together to finish. ✀

Gold Tapestry Mantel Scarf

By Carol Zentgraf

*Dress up your mantel for holiday or everyday with an elegant
corded scarf that reverses to suit your mood.*

Project Specifications

Skill Level: Beginner

Mantel Scarf Size: Approximately 55" x 19"

Note: *Materials are for 55" mantel. Adjust yardage as
needed for different-size mantels or fabric widths.*

Materials

- ⅝ yard each of two 56"–57"-wide coordinating
  decorator fabrics for alternating panels of one side
- ⅝ yard 56"–57"-wide decorator fabric for reversed
  side

- 2 yards of ½"-wide cord with lip
- 4 (3½") tassels to match cord
- Pattern tracing material 14" x 22"
- All-purpose threads to match fabrics
- Basic sewing supplies and tools

Instructions

Note: Use ½" seam allowance throughout and sew seams right sides together.

Step 1. Measure your mantel. This scarf is planned for a 55" mantel and is made up of five 11" panels. Adjust the panel width if necessary.

Step 2. Referring to Fig. 1, draw a panel pattern on pattern tracing material, adjusting size if necessary.

Step 3. Use panel pattern to cut three panels of one fabric and two of the coordinating fabric. Sew side edges of panels together, alternating fabrics. Press seams open.

Step 4. Place pieced scarf on reverse-side fabric. Pin in place and use as pattern to cut reverse side.

Step 5. Place scarf pieces right sides together with cord between on scalloped edge, lip aligned with raw edges. Pin all edges and stitch around perimeter, leav-

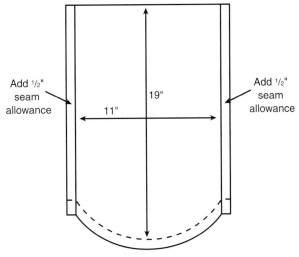

Add ½" seam allowance

Add ½" seam allowance

19"

11"

Fig. 1
Draw panel pattern as shown.

ing 8" opening in top straight edge. Clip curves and turn right side out. Close opening with hand stitches.

Step 6. Topstitch ½" from scalloped edge.

Step 7. Cut and knot the hanging loop on each tassel. Trim excess loop. Hand-tack top of each tassel to inward curves of alternating fabrics at each seam line to finish. ✂

Celebration Mantel Cover

By Marian Shenk

We love to decorate our mantels for holidays and special occasions.
Planning two sides of one cover saves time and money—and storage space!

Project Specifications

Skill Level: Beginner

Mantel Scarf Size: Approximately 50" x 8½" (12" drop)

Materials

For Spring Side

- 1 strip each off-white print 10½" x 50½" and 9" x 50½"
- Scraps of light and dark orchid and light and dark green prints for appliqué
- ⅜ yard purple print
- 2¾ yards of 1" green-and-orchid border print cut with ¼" seam allowance each side of stripe
- ½ yard brown narrow bias tape
- ¼ yard fusible transfer web
- 7 (2") gold tassels
- Clear nylon monofilament
- All-purpose threads to match fabrics
- Basic sewing supplies and tools

For Christmas Side

- ½ yard red Christmas print
- ½ yard green print
- 6½ yards ½"-wide green-and-gold metallic ribbon
- All-purpose threads to match fabrics
- Gold metallic thread
- Basic sewing supplies and tools

Instructions

Spring Side

Step 1. From purple print cut seven squares 5½" x 5½". Turn under ¼" on two adjacent sides of each square as shown in Fig. 1; press.

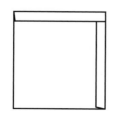

Fig. 1
Turn under ¼" on 2 adjacent sides of each square as shown.

Step 2. Place 10½" x 50½" strip of off-white print fabric on work surface. Place purple print squares diagonally along bottom of strip as shown in Fig. 2. Corners should touch and top corners should be 4½" from top edge of strip. Topstitch two folded edges of each square to muslin strip. Trim any muslin that extends below squares.

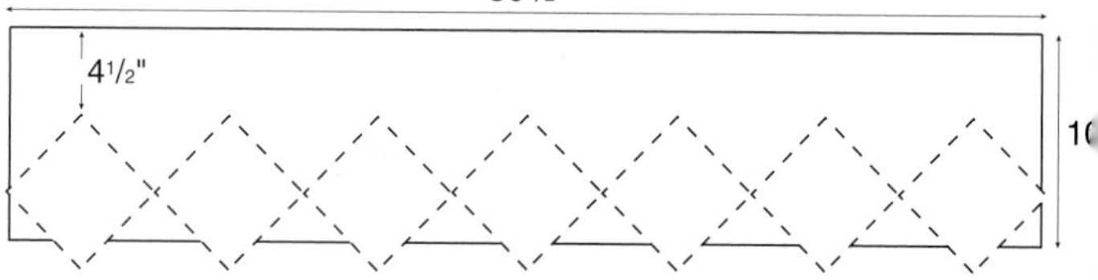

Fig. 2
Place squares along strip as shown.

Step 3. Cut six 3" strips of brown narrow bias tape. Position between each purple square for flower stem as shown in Fig. 3. Appliqué in place by hand or machine.

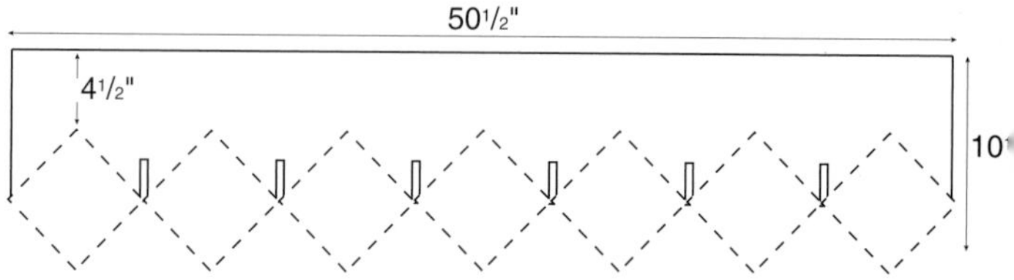

Fig. 3
Position flower stems as shown.

Step 4. Trace flower and leaf appliqués on paper side of fusible transfer web as directed on patterns. Cut out leaving roughly ¼" margin around traced lines.

Step 5. Following manufacturer's directions, fuse each appliqué to selected fabric. Cut out on traced lines. Referring to photo for placement on stems, arrange appliqués and fuse.

Step 6. Machine-appliqué around each shape with small satin stitch, using clear nylon monofilament in needle and matching all-purpose thread in bobbin.

Step 7. From 1½" green-and-orchid border stripe cut fourteen 7" pieces. Right sides facing, align each strip with lower raw edges of purple squares and stitch. Fold and miter each strip at each peak; pin. With clear nylon monofilament in needle and matching all-purpose thread in bobbin, stitch a narrow zigzag stitch over each miter to secure as shown in Figure 4.

Step 8. Right sides together, sew the 9" x 50½" strip of off-white print to the top of the appliquéd strip. Press seam allowance toward 9" strip.

Christmas Side

Step 1. From red Christmas print cut seven strips 2¾" x 13". From green print cut two strips 3⅜" x 13" and six strips 5¼" x 13". Sew together as shown in Fig. 5.

Step 2. From red Christmas print cut and piece two strips 3½" x 50½" and one green print strip 3½" x 50½". Sew red strips to each side of green strip on long edges. Press seam allowances toward green strip.

Step 3. Right sides facing, sew strip made in Step 2 to top of strip made in Step 1. Press seam allowance toward long red strip.

Step 4. From ½"-wide green-and-gold metallic ribbon cut fourteen 13" pieces. Pin one piece over each red/green vertical seam. Edge-stitch each side of ribbon with gold metallic thread.

Fig. 4
Zigzag over each miter to secure.

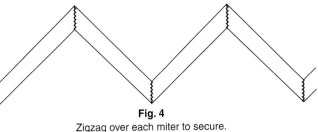

3⅜" 2¾" 5¼"   3⅜"

13"

Fig. 5
Sew strips together as shown.

Step 5. From ½"-wide green-and-gold metallic ribbon cut one 50½" length. Center over seam connecting the two long sections. Edge-stitch each side of ribbon with gold metallic thread.

Finishing

Step 1. Pin two mantel covers together, right sides facing and aligning top edges. Trim Christmas side to match points of spring side. Trim ends to same length.

Step 2. Sew around perimeter leaving 8" opening at top center. Clip corners and turn right side out; press.

Step 3. Close opening with hand stitches; stitch one gold tassel to each point to finish. ✄

Celebration Mantel Cover
Spring Flower Center
Cut 6 light orchid

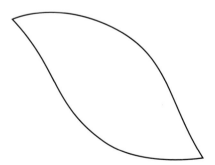

Celebration Mantel Cover
Spring Flower Leaf
Cut 12 dark green (reverse 6)
Cut 12 light green (reverse 6)

Celebration Mantel Cover
Spring Flower
Cut 6 dark orchid

Garden Place Mat

By June Fiechter

Why limit your spring place mats to short-time seasonal use
when you can flip them over for a new and different look in autumn?

Project Specifications

Skill Level: Beginner

Place Mat Size: Approximately 12" x 18"

Note: *Materials are for one place mat.*

Materials

- 2 off-white fabric rectangles 12" x 18"
- 1¾ yards purchased or self-made off-white bias binding
- Scraps of red, green and blue print fabric for appliqué
- Thin batting 12" x 18"
- Scraps of fusible transfer web
- Scraps of tear-away stabilizer
- All-purpose off-white thread
- Black machine-embroidery thread
- Black pearl cotton
- Couching presser foot for sewing machine
- Basic sewing supplies and tools

Instructions

Step 1. Gently round the corners of the off-white fabric

and batting rectangles to obtain oval shape. An existing place mat might be used as a pattern, or a small plate can be used to trace the curve.

Step 2. Trace all appliqué shapes on paper side of

fusible transfer web as instructed on patterns. Cut out leaving roughly ¼" margin around traced lines.

Step 3. Following manufacturer's instructions, fuse appliqué shapes to selected fabrics. Cut out on traced lines.

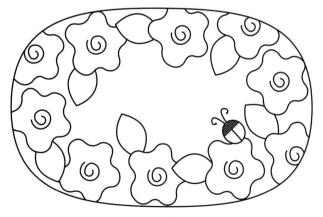

Fig. 1
Arrange spring side of place mat
roughly as shown.

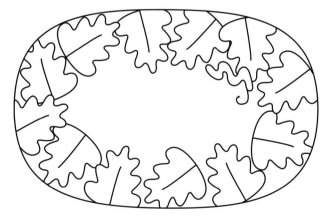

Fig. 2
Arrange autumn side of place mat
roughly as shown.

Step 4. Arrange flowers, leaves and ladybug on one oval as shown in Fig. 1; fuse. Arrange leaves and worm on second oval as shown in Fig. 2; fuse. Trim flower and autumn leaf edges as necessary at oval edge.

Step 5. Arrange black pearl cotton near edges of flowers, leaves, ladybug and worm. Couch the pearl cotton with a small, short zigzag stitch. Referring to photo, couch vein on autumn leaves and free-form squiggle in flower centers. Add one black pearl cotton antenna to worm and two antennae to lady-bug; couch.

Step 6. Place five pieces of black pearl cot-ton across top of ladybug very close together and place one piece vertically as shown in Fig. 3; couch.

Step 7. Place batting oval between two appliquéd ovals and pin-baste. Bind with off-white bias binding to finish. ✂

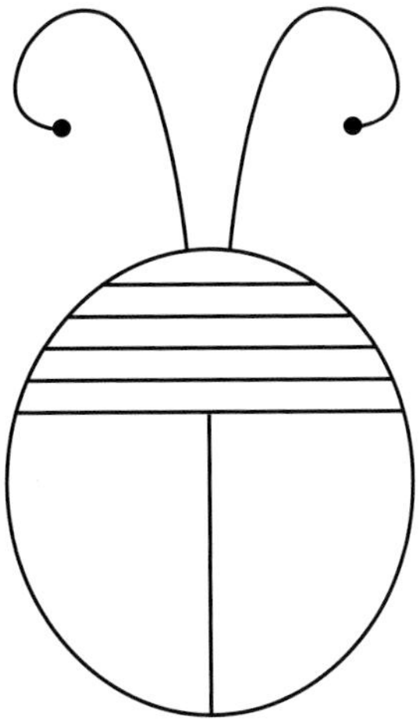

**Garden Place Mat
Ladybug**
Cut 1 red

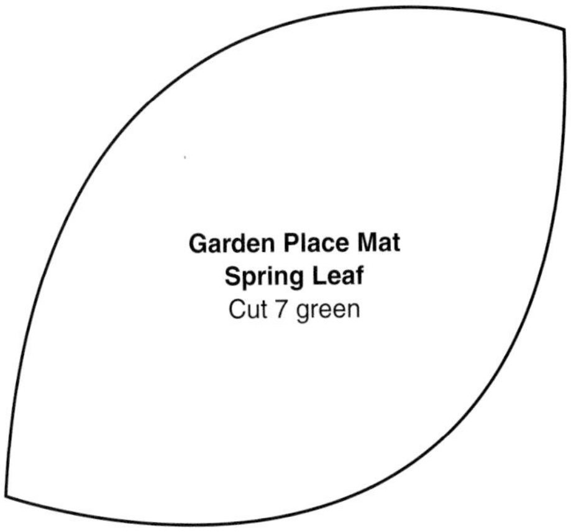

**Garden Place Mat
Spring Leaf**
Cut 7 green

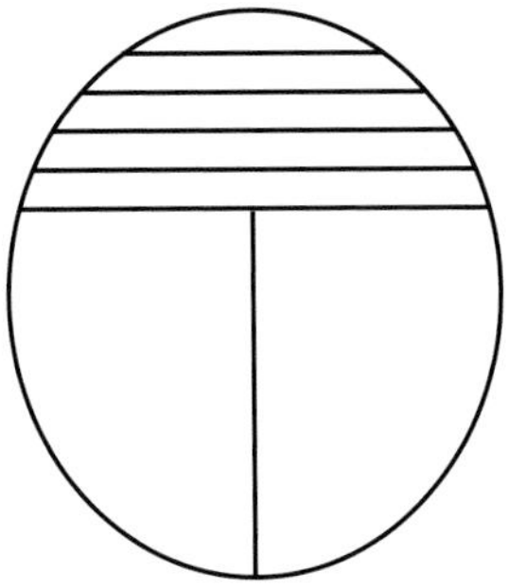

Fig. 3
Couch ladybug embellishment
as shown.

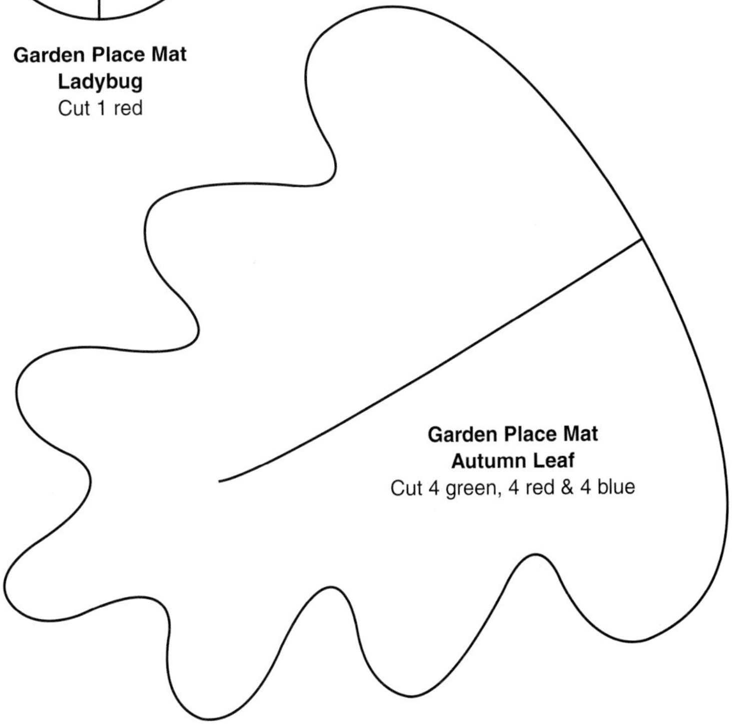

**Garden Place Mat
Autumn Leaf**
Cut 4 green, 4 red & 4 blue

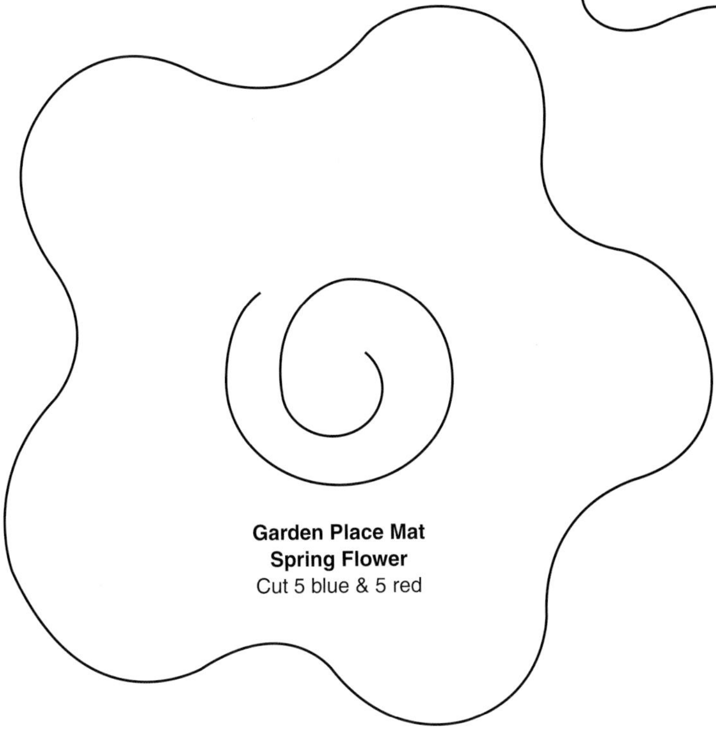

**Garden Place Mat
Spring Flower**
Cut 5 blue & 5 red

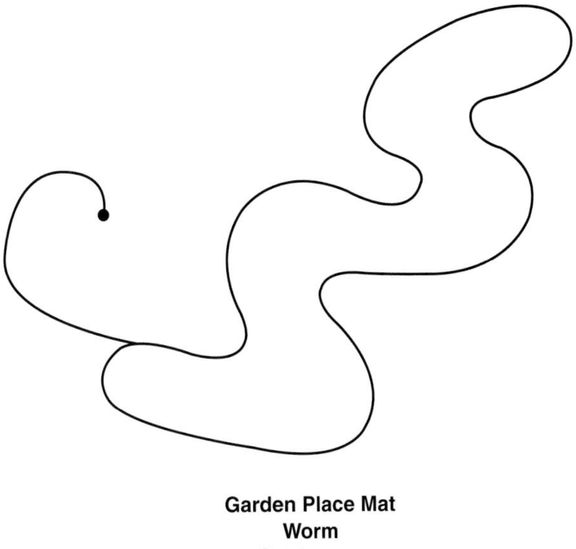

**Garden Place Mat
Worm**
Cut 1 green

Summer Fun Chair Covers

By Carol Zentgraf

*Dress up your ho-hum card-table chairs or lawn chairs for a summer party.
In fact, make it two parties with these terrific reversible covers!*

Project Specifications

Skill Level: Beginner

Size: Fits standard chairs with 15" x 15" seat and 17"-wide back

Note: *Materials will make covers for two chairs.*

Materials

- 2 yards striped 54"-wide decorator fabric
- 1⅛ yards 54"-wide coordinating print decorator fabric
- ⅓ yard 54"-wide coordinating solid decorator fabric
- 2 squares upholstery foam 15" x 15½"
- 4 yards of ½"-wide ribbon
- All-purpose threads to match fabrics
- Clear nylon monofilament
- Basic sewing supplies and tools

Instructions

Note: *Use ½" seam allowance throughout and sew all seams right sides together.*

Chair Cushions

Step 1. From striped and coordinating print fabrics cut two 17" x 17½" pieces each for chair cushions.

Step 2. From striped fabric cut four 3" x 21" and four 3" x 21½" strips with stripe running the length of strips for cushion bands. From coordinating solid fabric cut four 3" x 21" and four 3" x 21½" strips for reverse side of cushion bands.

Step 3. Find and mark centers of 21" solid-color cushion bands. Find and mark centers of 17" edges of striped cushion covers. Center and stitch in place, stopping and starting ½" from ends of cushion squares. Center and sew 21½" strips to 17½" sides of cushion. Miter corners and press seams open.

Step 4. Repeat Step 3, sewing striped bands to print cushion covers.

Step 5. Aligning seams, sew front and back panels together, leaving open on one side. Turn right side out and press. Press opening seam allowance under.

Step 6. With clear nylon monofilament, stitch in the ditch around center panel, leaving opening to correspond with edge opening. Insert foam cushion and topstitch the opening edge. Complete stitching in the ditch around center panel.

Step 7. Cut eight 8" pieces of ½"-wide

ribbon for cushion ties. Measure in 4" from topstitched edge and sew a ribbon end to each side of the cushion on the front and on the back. Place cushion on chair and tie to sides of chair.

Chair Backs

Step 1. From striped and coordinating print fabrics cut two back pieces each 17" x 22". From striped fabric cut four strips 5" x 22", stripes running the length of strip, for back bands.

Step 2. Sew one 22" band between two different chair backs on 22" edges. Press seams open. Bring short ends of strip together, right sides facing, and sew around remaining sides, leaving opening for turning. Turn right side out and close opening with hand stitches.

Step 3. On each side of chair back, make a ¾" buttonhole 4" from outside edge of band and 1" from side as shown in Fig. 1.

Step 4. Fold chair back in half crosswise, bringing one edge up to align with banded edge. Mark tie placement

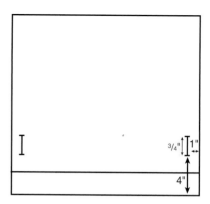

Fig. 1
Place and make buttonholes
as shown.

by marking through buttonhole to layer underneath.

Step 5. Cut eight 9" pieces of ½"-wide ribbon for cushion ties. Sew a ribbon length to front and back of cover at each buttonhole mark.

Step 6. Place folded cover over chair back with band in front. On each side, insert the front ribbon length through the buttonhole and tie into a bow with back ribbon length. ✂

Jungle Fever Shelf Cover

By Carol Zentgraf

Slipcover a basic shelving unit to put toys undercover. And you can change the whole look of the room with a flip to the reverse side.

Project Specifications

Skill Level: Beginner

Shelf Cover Size: Any size

Note: *Materials are for shelving unit 30" x 36" x 11", but yardage may be adjusted for other shelving sizes.*

Materials

- 3 yards each of two fabrics for cover
- 1 yard each of two fabrics for topper
- 1¼ yards coordinating stripe for bands and ties
- 2½ yards of pompom fringe
- 3 (¾") sets of sew-on hook-and-loop dots
- All-purpose threads to match fabrics
- Basic sewing supplies and tools

Instructions

Note: *Use ½" seam allowance throughout and sew seams right sides facing.*

Cover

Step 1. Measure the shelving unit width (w), depth (d) and height (h). Referring to Fig. 1, from each cover fabric cut two fronts, two sides, and one back. From one fabric only, cut one top.

Step 2. From coordinating stripe, cut four lower front bands, four lower side bands and two lower back bands. Also, from coordinating stripe, cut two 3"-wide strips equal to the full shelf height plus 1" for the front banding and four 3" x 20" strips for ties.

Step 3. To construct each cover, sew each lower band strip to corresponding cover piece. Sew front, sides and back of

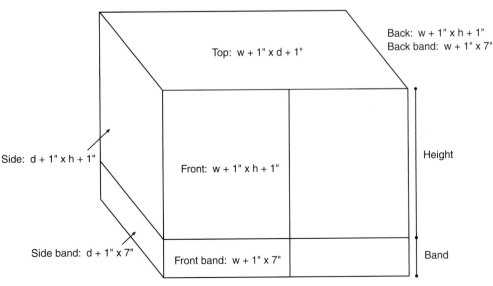

Back: w + 1" x h + 1"
Back band: w + 1" x 7"

Top: w + 1" x d + 1"

Side: d + 1" x h + 1"

Front: w + 1" x h + 1"

Height

Side band: d + 1" x 7"

Front band: w + 1" x 7"

Band

Fig. 1

each cover together, leaving the center front open. Press seams open.

Step 4. Pin the two covers together, right sides facing, aligning seams and edges. Sew together along bottom edges. Turn right side out and press.

Step 5. Baste upper and front edges of the covers together. Sew the cover upper edge to the cover top. *Note: The wrong side will show when the cover is reversed, but it will be covered by the topper.*

Step 6. Refer to instructions for Edge Finishes on page 26 for applying banding to finish the front edges and for tie closures. Space two ties on one side of each front, making sure they align before applying the band.

Step 7. On the side of front bands without ties, place one hook-and-loop dot at each tie location and one at top edge. Hand-sew dots to bands for a closure.

Topper

Step 1. Cut one top from each topper fabric the same size as instructed for cover top.

Step 2. From each topper fabric cut two 6"-wide strips equal to the shelf width plus 1" and two 6"-wide strips equal to the shelf depth plus 1".

Step 3. Sew depth and width strips of each fabric together as shown in Fig. 2. Right sides together, sew each band to its matching top.

Step 4. Place the two toppers together, right sides facing. Pin pompom fringe between layers. Sew around all edges, leaving opening for turning. Turn right side out and close opening with hand stitches to finish. ✂

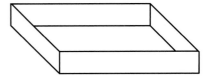

Fig. 2
Sew bands together as shown.

A Top for Every Jacket

By Carol Zentgraf

The perfect answer for packing light. Select fabrics carefully for a total of four different looks in one great garment!

Project Specifications

Skill Level: Beginner

Shell Size: Any size

Materials

- Commercial pattern for pullover shell top without darts
- 1 yard each of four different fashion fabrics
- Self-adhesive, double-sided basting tape
- All-purpose threads to match fabrics
- Basic sewing supplies and tools

Instructions

Note: *Although all pieces are fronts, the terms front and back will be used for clarity. Use ⅝" seam allowances throughout, right sides facing.*

Step 1. Use pattern front only and disregard any pattern facings. Cut one front from each fashion fabric.

Step 2. For shell front, sew two pieces together along armholes and neckline. Repeat for back. Press seams open.

Step 3. Turn back only right side out. Insert it between the layers of the front, aligning all edges. Sew the shoulder seams together. Turn the front right side out. You should have a front and back attached at the shoulders with a finished neckline and armholes.

Step 4. Sew the side seams of each shell. You will now have two completed shells with wrong sides together and an open lower edge.

Step 5. Press the lower edge of each shell to the wrong side, making sure the edges align. Secure the layers together with self-adhesive, double-sided basting tape, following manufacturer's instructions. Topstitch close to edges.

Step 6. If desired, topstitch the neckline and/or armholes. ✄

Flowers & Stripes Vest

By Marian Shenk

*Vests are versatile and are especially nice wardrobe extenders for travel.
Wear two different looks with one well-planned garment.*

Project Specifications

Skill Level: Beginner
Vest Size: Any size

Materials

Note: *Model was made in small size. Adjust yardage accordingly for other sizes.*

- McCalls vest pattern #2260, View D
- ¾ yard striped fabric
- ¾ yard coordinating floral print fabric

- ½ yard pink solid fabric to coordinate with print fabric
- 1 yard lightweight interfacing
- 3 yards of ½"-wide beige trim
- Embroidered appliqué for trim (approximately 3½" x 4½")
- All-purpose threads to match fabrics
- Basic sewing supplies and tools

Instructions

Step 1. From both fabrics and lightweight interfacing cut vest fronts and backs according to pattern directions.

Step 2. Right sides facing, sew striped vest together at shoulders and sides. Repeat with floral print vest and with interfacing vest.

Step 3. From floral print fabric cut one pocket. From pink solid fabric cut a 2" facing strip. Align right side of facing with back of pocket. Stitch across top with ¼" seam allowance. Bring facing to front of pocket. Fold under ¼" and pin to front of pocket. Cut ½"-wide beige trim the width of the facing. Hand-tack facing and trim to pocket.

Step 4. Fold rounded edge of pocket under ¼"; press. Place on left floral print vest front. Topstitch in place.

Step 5. Place two vests right sides together and interfacing on top of both. Sew around armholes. Turn right side out; press.

Step 6. From pink solid fabric, cut a 2" facing for around front, bottom and neck of vest. Sew facing together at shoulders and side seams; press.

Step 7. Pin right side of facing to striped side of vest and sew all around outside edge. Turn facing to print side of vest to hide raw edges; press.

Step 8. Turn inner edge of facing under ¼". Place ½"-wide beige trim over pressed edge; hand-tack facing and trim to vest, being careful not to stitch through to the striped side of vest.

Step 9. With hand stitches, sew embroidered appliqué to right side of striped vest to finish. ✂

Stylish Vest

By Ann Brown

Vests have become one of the most versatile items in today's wardrobe.

Make it reversible and you'll multiply all your outfits by two!

Project Specifications

Skill Level: Beginner

Vest Size: Any size

Project Notes

Select a vest pattern that has a V neckline and points at lower front (McCalls 8285 was used for model). The pattern should not be closely fitted. If pattern has darts, do not sew them. Select a coordinating or complementary fabric for lining because it, too, will be a wearable side if reversed. The instructions will refer to fashion fabric and lining fabric for clarity.

Materials

- Commercial vest pattern
- 8" x 14" piece of pattern tracing material
- Fashion fabric as directed by pattern
- Lining fabric as directed by pattern
- All-purpose threads to match fabrics
- 4 (⅞"–1") buttons
- Basic sewing supplies and tools

Instructions

Step 1. To add a fold-back lapel, tape pattern tracing material to front of pattern, extending beyond the front edge as shown in Fig. 1.

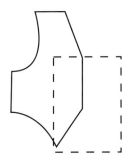

Fig. 1
Tape tracing material to pattern as shown.

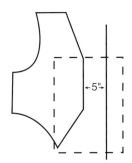

Fig. 2
Draw parallel line 5" from center front.

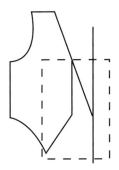

Fig. 3
Extend neck edge to meet parallel line.

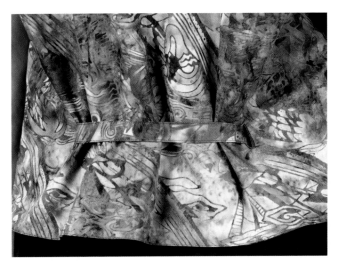

Step 2. Draw a line parallel to front edge of pattern 5" from center front as shown in Fig. 2.

Step 3. Extend V-neck edge to meet parallel line as shown in Fig. 3.

Step 4. At the point where the two lines intersect,

draw a line to the bottom point as shown in Fig. 4. Round the pointed edge as shown in Fig. 5. This adds a fold-back lapel to the vest pattern.

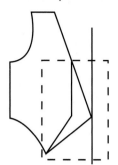

Fig. 4
Where 2 lines intersect, draw line to bottom point.

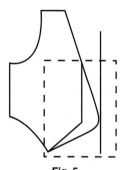

Fig. 5
Round pointed edge as shown.

Step 5. Cut two fronts and one back from fashion fabric and two fronts and one back from lining fabric. Right sides facing, sew each set together at side seams. Press seams open. If seams are serged, press seams toward front on one set and toward back on the other.

Step 6. Place one vest right side up on work surface. Place other vest on top, right sides facing. Leave a 5" opening along bottom back and sew around outside edges as shown in Fig. 6. Stop 1½" from shoulder. Sew

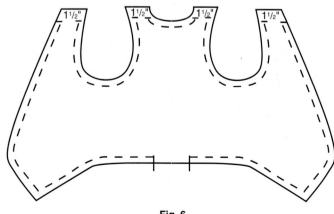

Fig. 6
Sew around vest edges as shown.

arm seam, starting and stopping 1½" from shoulder edges. Sew back neck edge, stopping and starting 1½" from shoulder edges. Trim seams to within ½" of sewn seam, clipping curves as needed. Do not trim seam allowances from unsewn areas.

Step 7. Turn vest right side out through 5" opening at back bottom; press seams. Reach up through opening in bottom edge and, holding lining front and back at shoulders, bring through opening.

Step 8. Sew lining together at shoulder seams as shown in Figure 7. Repeat for fashion side.

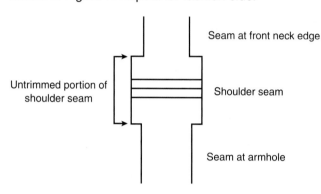

Fig. 7
Sew lining together at shoulder seams.

Step 9. Spread shoulder out; sew arm and neck edges closed. Pull back up through opening. Repeat for other side of vest.

Step 10. Press vest, turning seam allowance at opening toward inside of vest. Edge-stitch around the entire vest, which will close the opening and there will be no need for further hand sewing.

Step 11. Measure out 6" from either side of center back and 4½" up from bottom as shown in Fig. 8. This will mark the top of each buttonhole. Sew a 1" buttonhole at each marked position.

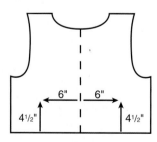

Fig. 8
Measure points as shown on vest back.

Step 12. Cut a 2½" strip across width of fashion fabric. Fold in half lengthwise, right sides facing. With ¼"

Continued on page 99

Americana Quilt

By Pearl Louise Krush

This is a sturdy quilt in an enduring theme. It's been designed for hard use and pleasure—both sides!

Project Specifications

Skill Level: Beginner
Quilt Size: Approximately 48" x 48"

Materials

- 3 yards navy plaid homespun
- 3 yards red plaid homespun
- 1 yard cream plaid homespun
- 1½ yards cotton batting
- 4 skeins cream 6-strand embroidery floss
- All-purpose cream thread
- Freezer paper or other pattern paper
- Rotary-cutting tools
- Basic sewing supplies and tools

Instructions

Step 1. Cut 36 squares each 10" x 10" from navy and red plaid homespun and cotton batting.

Step 2. Sandwich a batting square between a red and a navy plaid homespun square. Repeat for 36 blocks.

Step 3. Cut star appliqués as directed on pattern.

Step 4. Referring to photo for placement, lay out sandwiched squares in a checkerboard pattern, flipping sides for designated colors.

Step 5. Pin a cream plaid homespun star on each navy block.

Step 6. Carefully wind cream 6-strand embroidery floss on sewing machine bobbins

Step 7. Place a navy block with star appliqué on sewing machine. With cream all-purpose thread in needle and embroidery floss in bobbin, lower needle ¼" inside star outline and sew around star. Repeat for 18 blocks, leaving tail of thread and embroidery floss on each block. Pull floss up through all layers and clip thread and floss close to quilt.

Step 8. From freezer paper or pattern paper cut paper stars as directed on pattern. Pin or press on red squares. With cream all-purpose thread in needle and cream 6-strand embroidery floss in bobbin, stitch

around stars, through all layers, exactly on edge of cut star. Finish thread ends as in Step 7.

Step 9. Working with appliquéd blocks up, sew blocks in each row together, wrong sides facing, with 1" seam allowance and cream all-purpose thread in needle and bobbin. Seams will be on top of quilt. Sew rows together in the same way, with 1" seam allowance. Spread seam allowances apart at each intersection on each block to sew across.

Step 10. Make scant ¼" perpendicular clips to all seams as shown in Fig. 1. Repeat around outer edges of quilt.

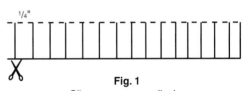

Fig. 1
Clip seams perpendicular
to stitching lines to fringe.

Step 11. Wash and then dry quilt in dryer. Remove lint often from dryer during drying process. Shake quilt vigorously outdoors to remove more lint and threads. Go over appliqué stars with masking tape to remove threads adhering to blocks. ✂

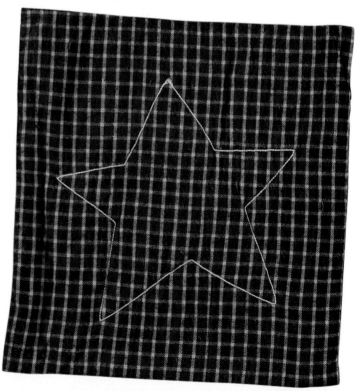

Americana Quilt Star
Cut 18 cream plaid homespun
on outer line for appliqué
Cut 18 paper stars on dashed
line for quilting pattern

Stylish Vest

Continued from page 96

seam allowance, stitch around three edges, leaving an opening on the long side for turning. Turn right side out, press and edge-stitch around entire piece for tie.

Step 13. Insert tie through buttonholes, draw up as needed to fit and tie as desired.

Step 14. Fold back the front lapel along center front. Determine placement for buttonholes and sew one on each lapel. Place buttons on fashion side and lining side of vest under lapel and sew. Button lapel in place as shown in Fig. 9. Repeat for remaining lapel to finish. ✂

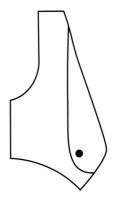

Fig. 9
Button lapel in place as shown.

Country Chickens Kitchen Set

By Pearl Louise Krush

A matched set of accessories will coordinate your kitchen—and when you flip them over for another look, you can have some fun!

Project Specifications

Skill Level: Beginner

Valance Size: Approximately 44" x 12" (including tabs)

Pot Holder Size: 10" x 10"

Place Mat Size: 14" x 20"

Basket Liner: 14" x 16"

Note: *Materials and instructions are for two place mats, two pot holders, one basket liner and one valance.*

Materials

- 1⅛ yards dark plaid homespun
- 1⅛ yards coordinating light stripe homespun
- 1 yard thin cotton batting
- 14 (⅞") buttons
- Scraps of fusible transfer web
- 8½" x 12" x 2" basket
- All-purpose threads to match fabrics
- Basic sewing supplies and tools

Instructions

Note: *Use ¼" seam allowance throughout.*

Valance

Step 1. Cut one 10" strip and one 1½" strip across the width of each homespun fabric. Using tab pattern, cut seven tabs from each of the homespun fabrics.

Step 2. Pin one 1½" homespun strip on opposite-color 10" strip 1½" from one long edge (bottom). Stitch ¼" from each long edge of 1½" strip. Repeat with remaining two strips.

Step 3. Place the two 10" valance strips right sides together. Sew both short sides and long top edge. Turn right side out and press.

Step 4. Stitch ¼" below decorative 1½" trim strip through both layers. Make ¼" cuts perpendicular to this stitching line all the way across the bottom edge of valance as shown in Fig. 1.

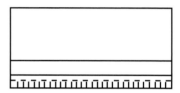

Fig. 1
Make ¼" cuts perpendicular to
stitching line to fringe.

ing every other tab to show opposite color. Pin one end of each tab to opposite sides of valance, overlapping 1"–1½". Place a ⅞" button on each end of each tab (front and back). Sew buttons in place connecting the tab to the back and front of the valance.

Step 7. Wash and then dry the valance. Use a needle or pin to separate the fringe along decorative strip and along bottom of valance.

Pot Holders

Step 1. Cut two 10" x 10" squares from each homespun fabric. Cut four 8" x 8" squares of thin cotton batting.

Step 2. Layer the two 8" x 8" thin cotton batting squares between two opposite-color homespun squares. Sew around perimeter 1" from cut edges and again 1¼". Repeat with remaining fabric and batting squares.

Step 3. Trace small chicken on paper side of fusible transfer web as instructed on pattern. Cut out leaving roughly ¼" margin around traced lines. Following manufacturer's instructions, fuse to dark plaid homespun. Cut out on traced lines. Fuse one chicken to light stripe homespun side of each pot holder; fuse.

Step 5. Place two tabs of opposite-color homespun right sides facing. Sew the long sides and bottom point. Clip the pointed seam area, turn right side out and press. Fold the raw top opening in ¼" and topstitch close to edge. Repeat for seven tabs.

Step 6. Space tabs evenly across top of valance, turn-

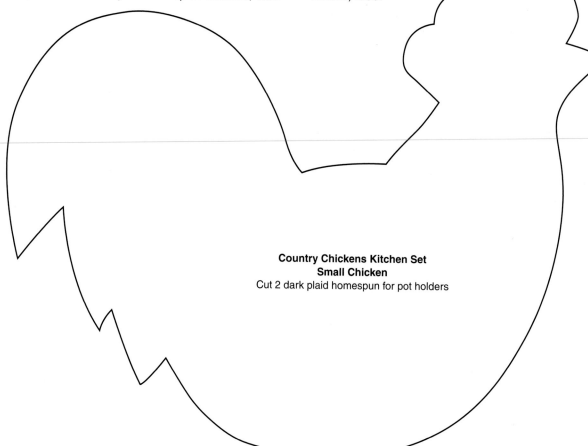

Country Chickens Kitchen Set
Small Chicken
Cut 2 dark plaid homespun for pot holders

Step 4. Machine-appliqué a satin stitch around each chicken shape. This stitching line will make a chicken shape on the reversed side of pot holder.

Step 5. Make perpendicular fringe cuts as in Valance Step 4. Wash, dry and fringe as in Step 7.

Place Mats

Step 1. Cut two rectangles 20" x 14" from each homespun fabric. Cut two 18" x 12" rectangles of thin cotton batting.

Step 2. Layer and stitch as in Pot Holders Step 2.

Step 3. Applique large chicken as in Pot Holder Steps 3 and 4.

Step 4. Make perpendicular fringe cuts as in Valance Step 4. Wash, dry and fringe as in Step 7.

Basket Liner

Step 1. Cut one rectangle 14" x 16" from each homespun fabric. Cut one rectangle 12" x 14" from thin cotton batting.

Step 2. Sew, appliqué and fringe as in pot holder and place mat projects using large chicken appliqué. ✂

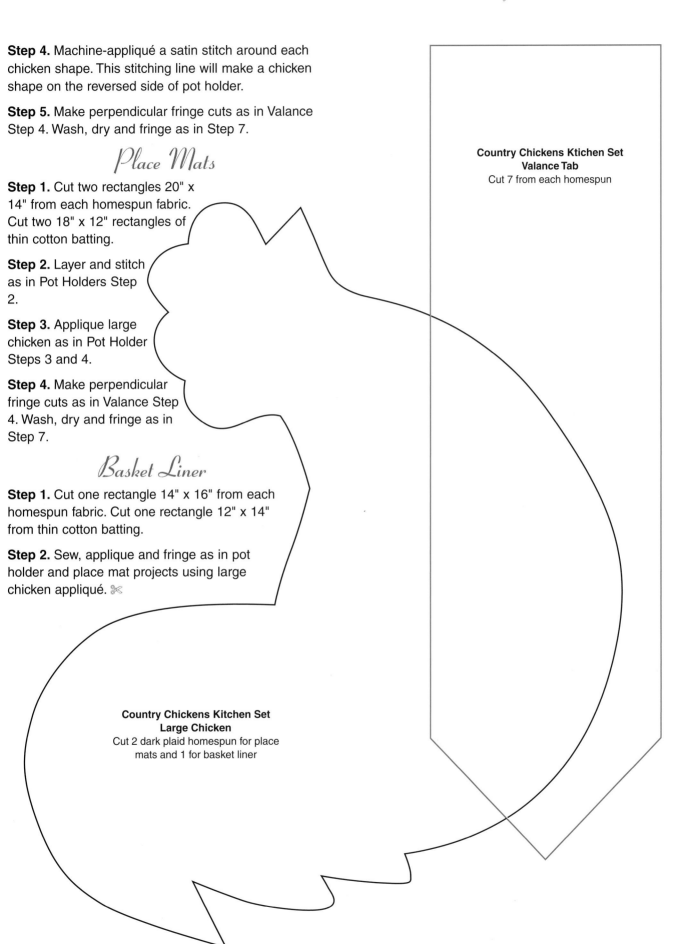

**Country Chickens Ktichen Set
Valance Tab**
Cut 7 from each homespun

**Country Chickens Kitchen Set
Large Chicken**
Cut 2 dark plaid homespun for place mats and 1 for basket liner

Oriental Fan

By Marian Shenk

Make this place mat in four different coordinating fabrics for a choice of very elegant looks for dining.

Project Specifications

Skill Level: Beginner

Place Mat Size: Approximately 22" x 12½"
(excluding tassel)

Materials

- ½ yard gold metallic butterfly print
- ¼ yard gold metallic leaf print
- ¼ yard gold-print solid-looking green fabric that coordinates with leaf and butterfly prints
- 5" x 10" darker green scrap that coordinates with butterfly print and leaf print
- 1¾ yards gold metallic quick bias
- 2½ yards gold metallic wide bias tape
- All-purpose threads that match fabrics
- Gold metallic thread
- 1 (3½") gold tassel
- Basic sewing supplies and tools

Instructions

Note: Use ¼" seam allowance throughout.

Step 1. Trace and cut fan blades as instructed on pattern. Sew together alternately as shown in photo.

Step 2. Trace and cut one large fan from gold metallic butterfly print.

Step 3. Trace and cut fan base shapes as instructed on pattern.

Step 4. Sew gold-print solid-looking green base to large fan shape and coordinating darker green base to pieced fan.

Step 5. Mark fan divisions between each scallop on large fan as shown on photo. Sew quick bias on each dividing line and over curved base seam with gold metallic thread in needle. Sew quick bias over curved base seam of pieced fan using gold metallic thread in needle.

Step 6. Use one completed fan shape to trace and cut batting. Sandwich layers with wrong sides of fans facing batting. Sew around perimeter close to edge.

Step 7. Bind raw edges with gold metallic bias tape. Attach the 3½" gold tassel to point with hand stitches to finish. ✄

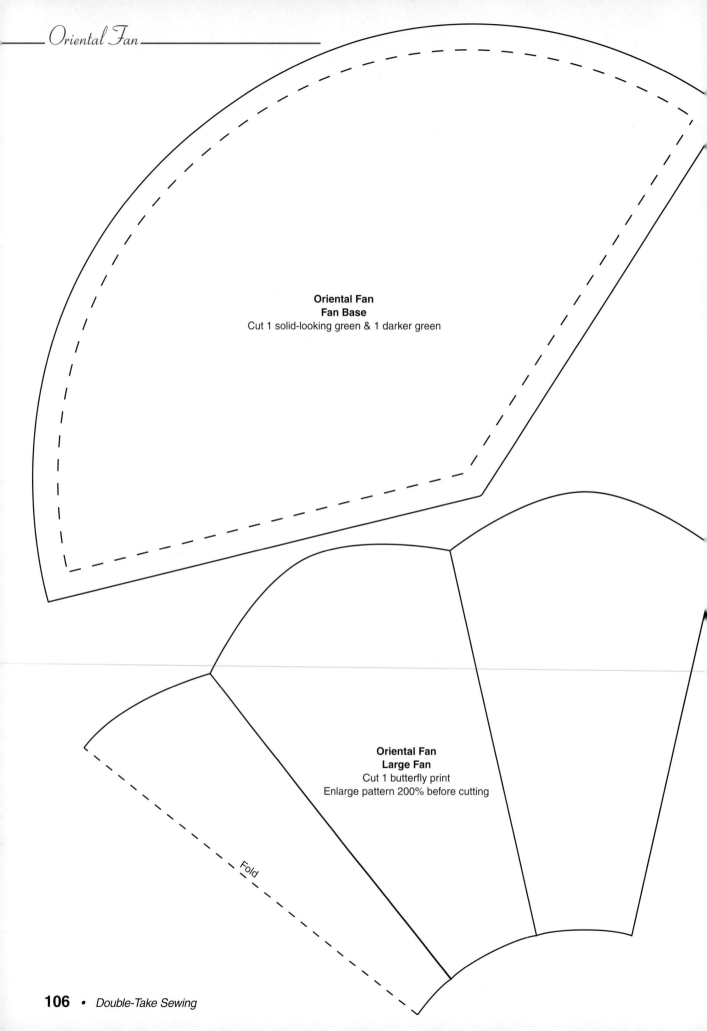

Oriental Fan
Fan Base
Cut 1 solid-looking green & 1 darker green

Oriental Fan
Large Fan
Cut 1 butterfly print
Enlarge pattern 200% before cutting

Fold

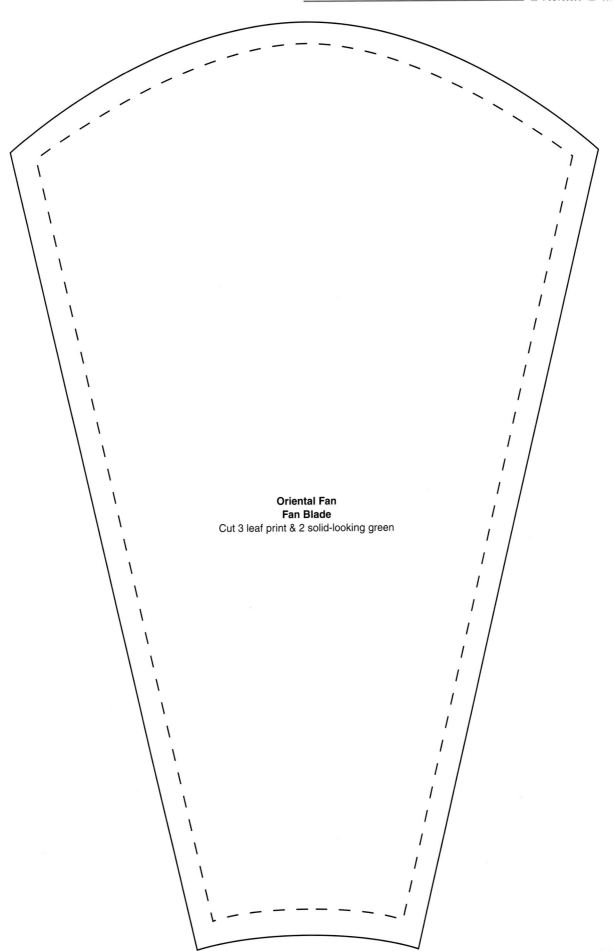

Oriental Fan
Fan Blade
Cut 3 leaf print & 2 solid-looking green

Casserole Cozy

By Carol Zentgraf

*Select a holiday theme fabric for each side of this handy accessory,
and you will be ready for all of your holiday entertaining.*

Project Specifications

Skill Level: Beginner

Cozy Size: Approximately 16" x 16"

Note: *Materials are for two-quart, 9¾" x 9¾" square casserole dish. Adjust materials as needed for other casserole sizes.*

Materials

- 17" x 17" square of Christmas print
- 17" x 17" square of autumn print
- 2¾ yards of 2½"-wide sheer wire-edge ribbon
- 2 fusible batting squares 17" x 17"
- 2 yards coordinating twisted cord with flange
- All-purpose threads to match fabrics
- Basic sewing supplies and tools

Instructions

Note: *Use ½" seam allowance throughout. For a*

different-size casserole dish, measure base plus sides for cozy width and base plus ends for cozy length. Add 3" to each measurement. Cut fabric and batting in determined dimensions.

Step 1. Layer and fuse both batting squares to wrong side of one 17" x 17" fabric square. Align all raw edges.

Step 2. Refer to Edge Finishes on page 26 and baste cord to edges of remaining fabric square. Mark a point 4" each side of each corner as shown in Fig. 1 for ribbon placement.

Step 3. Cut eight 12" lengths of 2½"-wide sheer wire-edge ribbon. Accordion-fold one ribbon end in quarters and baste to seam allowance at one mark, aligning raw edge of folded ribbon with raw edge of square. Repeat for eight ribbons, one at each mark.

Step 4. With batting on top and fabric squares facing,

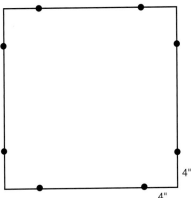

Fig. 1
Mark points on square as shown.

sew squares together leaving an opening for turning. Turn right side out and close opening with hand stitches.

Step 5. Center casserole dish on cozy and tie ribbons at each corner as shown in photo. ✂

Reversible Chair Pad

By Marian Shenk

Mix or match—whatever strikes your fancy on any given day! Just flip and retie for a different look.

Project Specifications

Skill Level: Beginner

Chair Pad Size: Approximately 19" x 16½"

Materials

- ½ yard each of two different coordinating fabrics
- 1 yard thick batting
- 2 yards contrasting wide bias tape that coordinates with both fabrics
- 20 (⅝") buttons (10 for each side, contrasting or matching)
- All-purpose threads to match each fabric
- Pattern paper
- Basic sewing supplies and tools

Continued on page 128

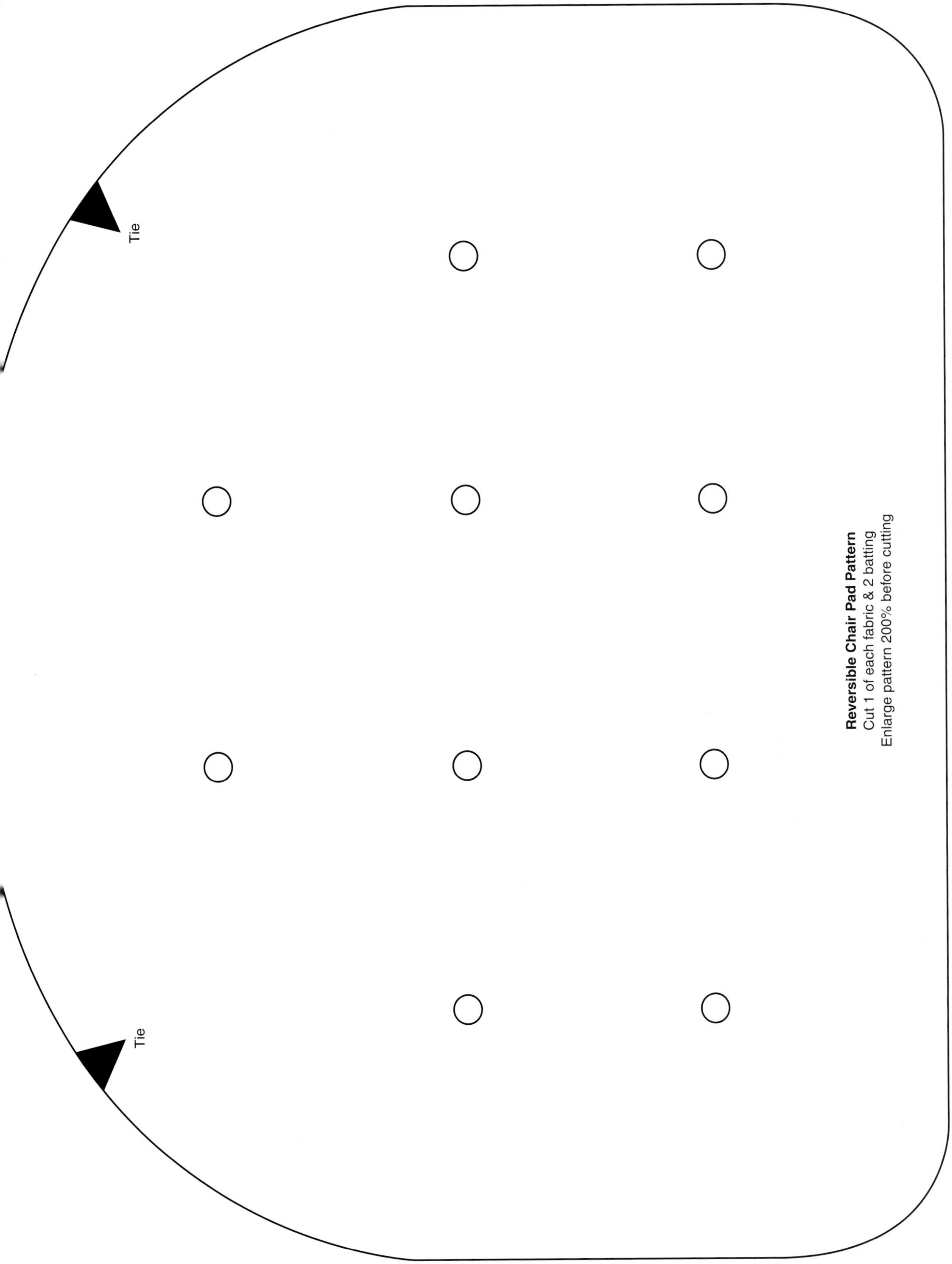

Tie

Tie

Reversible Chair Pad Pattern
Cut 1 of each fabric & 2 batting
Enlarge pattern 200% before cutting

Envelope Pillow

By Marian Shenk

With just a flip of the wrist, this lovely pillow assumes a new look and a change in your decor.

Project Specifications

Skill Level: Beginner

Pillow Size: Approximately 14" x 14"

Materials

- ½ yard floral decorator fabric
- ½ yard coordinating solid-color fabric
- Pillow form 14" x 14"
- 1¾ yard ⅜"-wide cord piping to match fabrics
- ¾ yard cord of smaller diameter to match larger cord piping
- 6 (1¼") buttons to cover
- All-purpose threads to match fabrics
- Basic sewing supplies and tools

Instructions

Step 1. From floral decorator fabric and coordinating solid color cut one square each 15" x 15". Enlarge flap pattern and cut as directed on pattern.

Step 2. Place flap pieces right sides facing and sew along short sides and scalloped edge. Clip corners and curves and turn right side out; press.

Step 3. Hand-sew smaller diameter cord to scalloped edge of flap.

Step 4. Place floral side of flap on one right edge of floral square and sew across.

Step 5. Sew ⅜"-wide diameter cord piping to right side of floral square along the three remaining sides.

Step 6. Place coordinating solid-color 15" x 15" square on floral square, right sides facing. Sew all around leaving an opening at lower edge for pillow insertion.

Step 7. Turn right side out through opening. Insert pillow and close opening with hand stitches.

Step 8. Cover three buttons with floral decorator fabric and three with coordinating solid-color fabric. Sew the plain buttons to the floral side of flap and the floral buttons to the solid side of flap. ✂

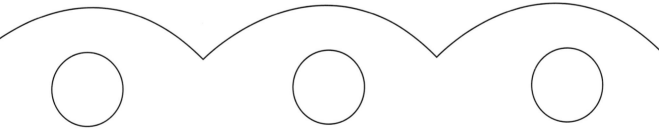

Envelope Pillow
Flap Pattern
Cut 1 floral & 1 solid
Enlarge pattern 200% before cutting

Lace-Up Window Treatment

By Carol Zentgraf

Not only does this shade reverse, but so does the valance—
for a potential of four different design combinations.

Project Specifications

Skill Level: Beginner

Shade Size: 36" x 34"

Valance Size: 53" x 12"

Note: *Adjust fabric, webbing, cord and interfacing yardage, number of grommets and length of mounting board for other window sizes.*

Materials

- ½ yard each of two different coordinating 54"-wide decorator fabrics for valance
- 1 yard each of two different coordinating 54"-wide decorator fabrics for shade
- 3" x 54" strip heavyweight fusible interfacing
- 4 yards coordinating 1"-wide webbing
- 4½ yards (¼") yellow ribbon
- 14 (1") grommets
- 36" x ¾"-wide mounting board
- Staple gun
- All-purpose threads to match fabrics
- Permanent fabric adhesive
- Basic sewing supplies and tools

Instructions

Note: *Use ½" seam allowance throughout.*

Shade

Step 1. To determine shade fabric measurements, measure window inside width and length. Add 1" to width and 2" to length. With these measurements cut one panel from each shade fabric.

Step 2. Place shade panels right side up on flat work surface. Measure in 9" from each side of each panel and mark for lengthwise webbing placement as shown in Fig. 1. Cut webbing to correct length and, following manufacturer's directions, use permanent fabric adhesive to adhere webbing to panels. Allow to dry thoroughly.

Step 3. Right sides facing, sew shade panels together

along side and lower edges. Turn right side out. Baste upper raw edges together. Staple upper edge to mounting board.

Step 4. Cut two 54" pieces of yellow ribbin. Center each piece over mounting board edge of shade at the webbing strip location. Staple to each side of mounting board.

Step 5. Screw shade mounting board into upper edge of window frame. Roll shade up to desired height and tie the cord ends to secure.

Valance

Step 1. To determine valance fabric width, measure window inside width and add ½ that measurement to width. For example, the featured window width is 36". Half that measurement is 18". Therefore, the valance fabric width is 54". Cut one panel from each fabric 13" x 54".

Step 2. Right sides facing, sew the two panels together leaving an opening on one short edge. Following manufacturer's instructions, fuse interfacing along upper edge of one panel. Turn right side out and press. Close opening with hand stitches.

Step 3. Following manufacturer's instructions, evenly space and apply the grommets to upper valance edge.

Step 4. Loop white cotton cord through grommet openings to hang valance from a decorative curtain rod as shown in photo. ✂

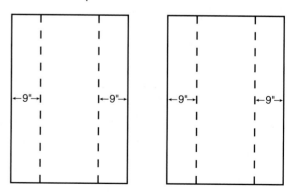

Fig. 1
Position webbing on fabric panels
as shown.

Button-Up Window Panels

By Carol Zentgraf

Plan to line tabbed window panels with a coordinating fabric and achieve two window treatments with half the time and money!

Project Specifications

Skill Level: Beginner

Panel Size: 24" x 42" (excluding tabs)

Note: *Two panels fit a window 44" x 41". Adjust yardage for other window sizes.*

Materials

- 3 yards 54"-wide toile decorator fabric
- 3 yards 54"-wide coordinating stripe decorator fabric
- 16 (1⅛") wooden buttons
- 4 (1⅝") wooden buttons
- All-purpose threads to match fabrics
- Basic sewing supplies and tools

Instructions

Note: *Use ½" seam allowance throughout.*

Step 1. To determine panel size, measure window and frame to determine the total window covering size needed. Panel edges should extend beyond the window opening to prevent light leakage. Divide width in half for each panel. Add 1" to width and 1" to length for seam allowances.

Step 2. From each fabric cut two panels in determined dimensions. Cut eight 3½" x 10" tabs from each fabric.

Step 3. Right sides facing, sew one 3½" x 10" tab of each fabric together along long edges and one end. Trim seams, clip corners and turn right side out; press. Stitch a vertical 1⅛" buttonhole ½" from finished end on each tab as shown in Fig. 1. Repeat for eight tabs.

Step 4. Evenly space and baste four tabs to upper edge of each toile panel, raw edges aligned.

Step 5. Right sides facing, sew one striped panel to one toile panel, stitching around perimeter and leaving an opening for turning. Turn right side out, press and close opening with hand stitches. Repeat for second panel.

Step 6. For each panel fold tabs down to overlap the panel edge 2½". Mark button placement. Reverse and mark on other side. Sew 1⅛" wooden buttons in place, one on each side of panel.

Step 7. Place panels on work surface side by side, aligning upper and lower edges. Fold the lower inside corner of each panel up as shown in Fig. 2. Mark and sew a vertical 1⅝" buttonhole. Position 1⅝" wooden button on each side of panel to match placement of buttonhole. Sew buttons in place to finish. ✄

Fig. 1
Make buttonhole on each tab as shown.

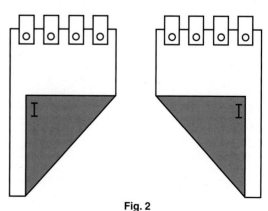

Fig. 2
Fold each panel up as shown and make buttonhole.

Prairie Points Vest

By Carol Zentgraf

Contrasting piping and prairie points add special visual interest to a simple reversible vest.

Project Specifications

Skill Level: Beginner
Vest Size: Any size

Materials

- Commercial vest pattern
- Fabric yardage as indicated on pattern—one fabric for each side of vest
- ¼ yard coordinating fabric for prairie points

- ½ yard different coordinating fabric to cover piping
- Cotton cord for piping in length to go around all edges (not armholes)
- All-purpose threads to match fabrics
- Basic sewing supplies and tools

Instructions

Note: *Use ⅝" seam allowance.*

Step 1. Follow pattern guide sheet to cut vest fronts and back from each fabric. Eliminate center front seam allowance and facings.

Step 2. Measure around front and lower vest edges to determine piping length. Refer to Edge Finishes, page 26, to create piping and a strip of prairie points equal to this same length.

Step 3. Baste piping to the prairie points, aligning the outer finished piping edge with the inward V of the points.

Step 4. For each vest layer sew the fronts to the back at the shoulder seams. Press the seams open. Baste the prairie points/piping to the outer edges of one vest layer.

Step 5. Sew the layers together along the neckline, front, armhole and lower edges, leaving the sides open.

Step 6. Pull the layers of one vest through the opposite vest opening and sew each front to the back. For the remaining side, work through the opening to sew the front and back of one layer together. Press under the seam allowances on the remaining opening and close opening with hand stitches.

Step 7. If necessary to reduce bulk at the lower edge side seam, open the seam and trim excess piping/prairie points. Overlap or butt the piping edges together and slipstitch in place. ✄

Fall/Winter Jacket

By June Fiechter

Why line a jacket with a boring lining fabric when you can just as easily make the jacket reversible? Two for the price of one!

Project Specifications

Skill Level: Beginner
Jacket Size: Medium

Materials

- 1⅓ yards pastel plaid flannel for fall side of jacket
- 1 rectangle 18" x 17¼" coordinating solid-color fleece for winter jacket back
- 1¼ yards second coordinating solid-color fleece for winter jacket fronts and sleeves
- ¼ yard white fleece for snowdrifts and appliqué
- Light tan fake leather for acorns 8" x 9" and 5" x 5"
- Scraps of coordinating fake leather, suede or fleece for patches
- 10 (½") matching buttons
- Permanent fabric adhesive
- Brown and gold 6-strand embroidery floss
- Coordinating or contrasting 6-strand embroidery floss or fake leather yarn to sew patches
- Embroidery needle
- Water-soluble marker
- Scraps of fusible transfer web
- Basic sewing supplies and tools

Instructions

Fall Jacket

Note: *Use ¼" seam allowance throughout.*

Step 1. From pastel plaid flannel cut two rectangles 18" x 22". These are the body front and back pieces. Place pieces together on work surface, right sides facing. Pin together, leaving a 9" space at each side at the top for sleeve holes. Stitch pieces together at sides and shoulders, leaving a 7¼" opening at center top as shown in Fig. 1.

Step 2. Mark and cut a slit up center front. Use V-neck pattern to cut V-shaped

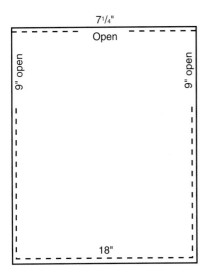

Fig. 1
Stitch front and back pieces
together as shown.

Stitch around edges with a running stitch and 3 strands of contrasting 6-strand embroidery floss.

Step 8. Position and fuse cap of large acorn as shown in photo. Glue base of acorn by running a line of permanent fabric adhesive around curved edges only. Leave unattached along top for pocket entry.

Step 9. Bind top of pocket with buttonhole stitch and 3 strands of contrasting 6-strand embroidery floss. Work running stitch around remaining outside edges of

neckline at center front. Press and turn inside out.

Step 3. Prepare sleeve pattern and cut two sleeves from pastel plaid flannel. Fold each sleeve, right sides together, and sew seams. Turn right sides out and pin sleeves to openings with right sides facing. Sleeve caps will be slightly gathered. Sew each sleeve in place; press.

Step 4. Cut two sleeve patches from scraps of coordinating fake leather, suede or fleece 2¼" x 2¼" and 2½" x 2½". Cut two patches 2½" x 2½" and one patch 3" x 3" for jacket right front.

Step 5. Trace large and small acorns on paper side of fusible transfer web. Cut out acorns, leaving roughly ¼" margin around traced lines. Following manufacturer's directions, fuse to light tan fake leather. Cut out on traced lines.

Step 6. Position sleeve and jacket right front patches as shown in photo. Secure with buttonhole stitch or other decorative embroidery stitch using 3 strands of contrasting 6-strand embroidery floss. Tie two small bows with 6-strand embroidery floss or fake leather yarn. Attach one bow to a sleeve patch and one to a front patch.

Step 7. Position small acorn over right front patches as shown in photo. Fuse lower part of acorn with cap overlapping.

acorn. Trim large acorn with a small bow as in Step 6. Sew two ½" buttons to edge of pocket as shown in photo and one ½" button to a right front patch.

Winter Side

Step 1. From pastel plaid flannel cut one yoke piece 5¼" x 18". Sew 18" edge to 18" x 17¼" coordinating solid-color fleece for jacket back. These pieces joined make the 18" x 22" jacket back.

Step 2. From second coordinating solid-color fleece cut one rectangle 17" x 18". Place on work surface and draw a snowdrift line on lower 18" edge as shown in Fig. 2. Cut on drawn line.

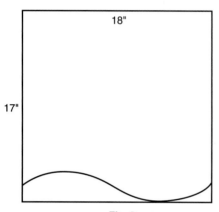

Fig. 2
Draw snowdrift line as shown.

Step 3. From white fleece cut one rectangle 8" x 18". Use cut-off fabric from Step 2 as pattern to mark top of snowdrift on white fleece rectangle. Cut on line. Place on bottom edge of rectangle shaped in Step 2 and sew in place with buttonhole stitch and 3 strands of contrasting 6-strand embroidery floss.

Step 4. If necessary, trim lower edge so that front and back rectangles measure 18" x 22". Repeat Fall Jacket, Steps 1–3.

Step 5. Trace four snowflakes and snowman appliqué pieces on paper

side of fusible transfer web. Cut out leaving roughly ¼" margin around traced lines. Following manufacturer's instructions, fuse to selected fabrics, referring to photo for ideas.

Step 6. Referring to photo, position and fuse to jacket. Work buttonhole stitch around all edges with 3 strands of matching or contrasting 6-strand embroidery floss. Also work buttonhole stitch along lower edge of back yoke.

Step 7. Satin-stitch twig snowman arms with 3 strands of brown embroidery floss. Satin-stitch nose with 3 strands of gold floss. Work French knots in contrasting color for eyes.

Step 8. Sew ½" button to center of each flower and three to front of snowman referring to photo for placement.

Assembly

Step 1. Place right sides of both jackets together and seam the front slit, the V and the neck hole. Turn right side out; press.

Step 2. Push sleeves through with flannel as lining. Place on work surface. Flatten and straighten the jacket. Bring the end of the flannel sleeve back up and over the winter jacket sleeve for a cuff at the sleeve opening. Press raw edge under and secure with buttonhole stitch using 3 strands of the same color embroidery floss used to stitch yoke.

Add 11¾" between sleeve bottom and top to make complete pattern

Cut solid fabric to this line

Place on fold

**Fall/Winter Jacket
Sleeve Bottom**

Cut plaid fabric to this line

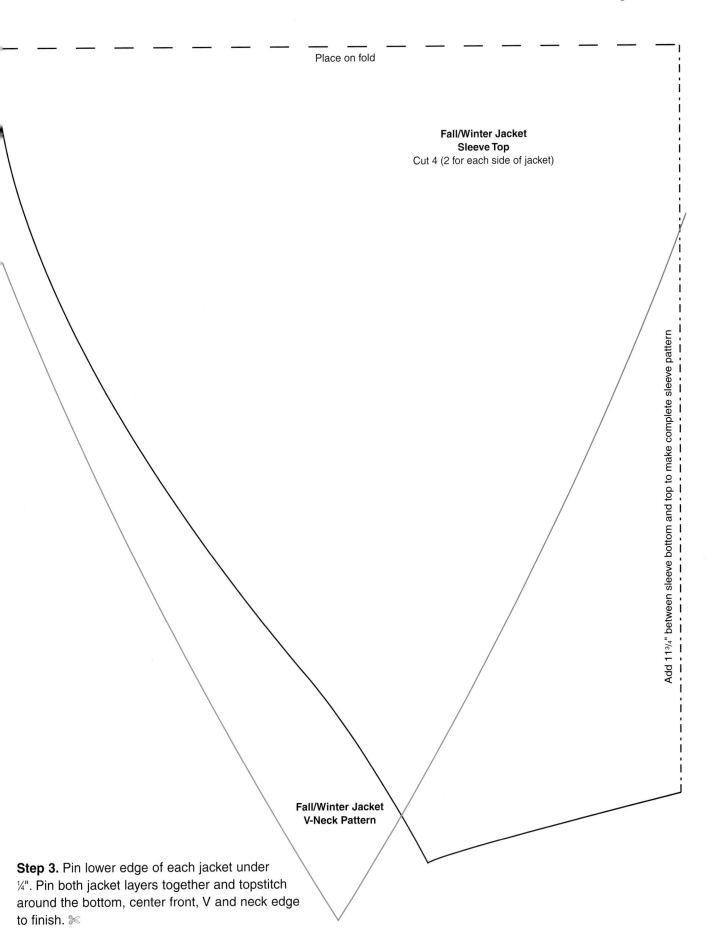

Place on fold

Fall/Winter Jacket
Sleeve Top
Cut 4 (2 for each side of jacket)

Add 11³/₄" between sleeve bottom and top to make complete sleeve pattern

Fall/Winter Jacket
V-Neck Pattern

Step 3. Pin lower edge of each jacket under
¼". Pin both jacket layers together and topstitch
around the bottom, center front, V and neck edge
to finish. ✂

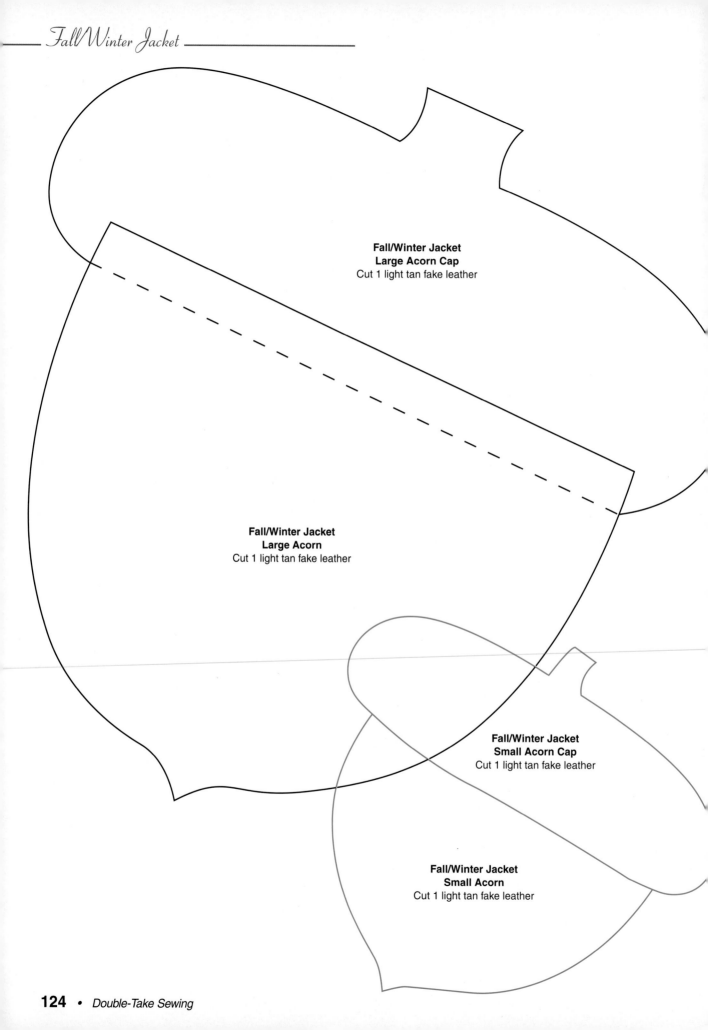

Fall/Winter Jacket
Large Acorn Cap
Cut 1 light tan fake leather

Fall/Winter Jacket
Large Acorn
Cut 1 light tan fake leather

Fall/Winter Jacket
Small Acorn Cap
Cut 1 light tan fake leather

Fall/Winter Jacket
Small Acorn
Cut 1 light tan fake leather

**Fall/Winter Jacket
Snowman**

**Fall/Winter Jacket
Snowflake**
Cut 4 white fleece

Peekaboo Vest & Hat

By Carol Zentgraf

The proud owner of this vest doesn't need a magic wand to change the colors of her hat and vest!

Project Specifications

Skill Level: Beginner

Jacket Size: Any size

Hat Size: Any size

Materials

- Child's fleece vest and hat pattern
- Fleece in each of two colors as indicated for size on commercial pattern
- Interfacing as required
- Zipper as required
- Fusible tear-away fabric stabilizer
- Self-adhesive, double-sided basting tape
- Decorative-edge fabric scissors
- Pattern paper
- Dual-purpose threads to match fabrics
- Basic sewing supplies and tools

Instructions

Note: *Use ¼" seam allowances throughout.*

Vest

Step 1. Follow pattern instructions to cut the vest and hat pieces from each fleece color, disregarding any interfacings.

Step 2. Trace and cut a variety of heart and star shapes from pattern paper. Arrange on one left front and one right front of one fleece color, referring to photo for placement ideas. The number and placement may vary for different sizes. The star and heart areas should not overlap.

Peekaboo Vest & Hat
Heart Pattern
Cut various sizes as needed

Step 3. Trace all the patterns on the fabric stabilizer. Cut out adding ½" to all traced lines.

Step 4. Following manufacturer's instructions fuse hearts only to left and right fronts of one fleece color. Cut and fuse a square of tear-away fabric stabilizer larger than each heart to the wrong side of the fabric behind each heart. On the right side stitch around the edge of each heart ¼" from the traced edge. Leaving the stabilizer in place until after the layers are assembled, cut out each heart ¼" inside the stitched line.

Step 5. Repeat Step 4 with stars only on left and right fronts of the second color of fleece.

Step 6. For each colored layer, sew the fronts to the backs at the shoulder seams. Refer to Closing Time on page 44 and follow the second technique for applying an exposed zipper in a double-layer garment.

Step 7. Remove the tear-away fabric stabilizer from the wrong sides only of each color. Apply double-sided basting tape along the edges of each cutout. Turn the layers right side out. Align all edges and press the cutout edges firmly to adhere to the reverse layer. Make certain the fabric is smooth on both sides.

Step 8. Stitch around each cutout on the existing stitching line to sew it to the other layer. Remove stabilizer from the right sides of each color.

Step 9. For each layer, sew the side seams together. Topstitch the layers together ½" from the armhole edges and 1" from the lower edges. Trim the raw edges with decorative-edge scissors

Hat

Step 1. Follow the pattern guide sheet to make one hat from each color. Do not finish the lower edges.

Step 2. Place one hat inside the other, wrong sides facing and staggering the band seams to reduce bulk.

Step 3. Add one heart and one star cutout to the hat brim in the same manner as the vest.

Step 4. Topstitch the lower edges of the two layers together ½" from the edge. Trim the edge with decorative-edge scissors. ✂

Peekaboo Vest & Hat
Star Pattern
Cut various sizes as needed

Reversible Chair Pad

Continued from page 110

Instructions

Step 1. Enlarge and make chair pad pattern using pattern paper. Trace and cut chair pad pieces as directed on pattern.

Step 2. Cut two fabric strips 1" x 12" from each fabric. Fold raw 12" edges under ¼", then fold each strip in half lengthwise. Topstitch folded edges to form four ties.

Step 3. Pin one tie of each fabric, one on top of the other, on one fabric at positions indicated on pattern.

Step 4. Place one fabric right side down on work surface. Place two batting pieces on top and place other fabric piece right side up on top. Baste around edges.

Step 5. Bind edges with contrasting wide bias tape.

Step 6. Mark positions for 10 buttons on one side of cushion as indicated on pattern. Position other set of buttons in exactly the same places on reverse side of cushion. Sew buttons in place through all layers and through both buttons. Pull tightly to tuft. ✂

Country Jumper

By Holly Daniels

*Appliqué kittens and puppies on one side for fun, then reverse
to a sprinkling of spring flowers for a dressier look.*

Project Specifications

Skill Level: Beginner

Jumper Size: Any size

Note: *Model is size 8. Adjust fabric amounts for other
sizes as required by pattern. Dark side of denim will be
used for appliqué side of jumper and the lighter
(reverse) side of denim will be used for the floral jumper.*

Materials

- Simplicity jumper pattern 7190
- 2 yards lightweight blue denim
- Scraps of light, medium and dark tan for
  cat and dog appliqués
- Scraps of rust-and-tan check for dog ears
  and light-and-dark-tan check for cat ears
- 8 rectangles of rust plaid 6½" x 3½"
- 2¼ yards medium-blue self-made or
  purchased piping
- Dark brown 6-strand embroidery floss
- 2½ yards pink baby rickrack
- 2½ yards blue baby rickrack
- Embroidery needle
- 2 (¾") blue buttons
- 2 (¾") pink buttons
- All-purpose threads to match fabrics
- Clear nylon monofilament
- Light pink, dark pink and yellow machine-
  embroidery threads
- Embroidery hoop for machine-applique
- Template plastic scrap
- Freezer paper
- Air-soluble marker
- Fabric stabilizer
- Basic sewing supplies and tools

Instructions

Pattern Preparation

Step 1. Prepare the jumper pattern by adjusting the
skirt length so that the hem is only ¼" deep.

Step 2. Measure around the bottom of the skirt pattern. If the measurement is more or less than 73¼", adjust the width of the skirt equally between front and back pieces for a total measurement of 73¼". If the jumper is made in a much smaller size, you may adjust the bottom appliqué band by reducing the size of plaid panels, reducing the number of appliqués or both. Use bodice pattern as provided, disregarding ties and pockets.

Floral Side

Note: If you prefer, you may substitute premade floral appliqués for machine-embroidered flowers.

Step 1. From lightweight blue denim cut one skirt front, one skirt back, two bodice backs and one bodice front. Trace second bodice front onto light side of one piece of denim with air-soluble marker. Cut out leaving 2"–3" margin on all sides to accommodate hoop during machine embroidery.

Step 2. From fabric stabilizer cut one bodice front the same size as denim bodice front to be embroidered. Attach to reverse side of bodice with pins or light basting.

Step 3. Transfer 14 flower patterns randomly to right side of bodice front with air-soluble marker. Machine-

Light Pink

Flower Foundation   Circular Stitch

Flower Stitch Pattern
Make foundation by stitching
each petal with circular stitch.

Dark Pink
Petals
Start in center. Stitch out,
then back to center on petals.

Yellow

Circular Stitch for Flower Center

Finished Flower

Fig. 1
Machine-embroider flowers as shown.

embroider as shown in Fig. 1. Cut bodice on traced pattern lines.

Step 4. Sew skirt front and back together with flat-felled seam as shown on page 15.

Step 5. Use air-soluble marker to draw a line ¾" from lower raw edge of skirt. Draw a second line 3" from lower raw edge. Mark 6" intervals along each line as shown in Fig. 2. Then mark alternating points at 6" intervals between two lines. Position pink and blue baby rickrack on marks, pivoting at upper and lower marks and crossing at points in between as shown in Fig. 3. Stitch rickrack with matching threads.

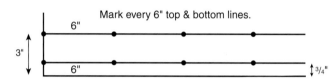

Mark every 6" top & bottom lines.

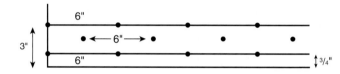

Fig. 2
Mark lower edge of jumper as shown.

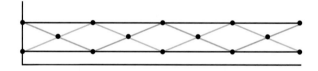

Fig. 3
Rickrack will pivot on top and bottom row marks
and cross at marks on middle row.

Step 6. Transfer one flower pattern to center of each diamond formed by rickrack placement. Baste or pin fabric stabilizer to reverse side of each embroidery area. Machine-embroider as in Step 3.

Appliquéd Side

Step 1. Trace dog and cat ear patterns on template plastic scrap; cut out. Fold rust-and-tan checked fabric for dog ears right sides together. Trace eight dog ears on wrong side of top fabric. Do not cut out. Machine-stitch around traced ear shapes, through both fabric layers, leaving open on one side as designated on pattern. Cut out ears, leaving ⅛" seam allowances. Turn right side out; press. Fold light-and-dark tan check and trace 10 cat ears. Continue as for dog ears.

Step 2. Trace five cat heads, four dog muzzles and four dog heads on unwaxed side of freezer paper. Cut out on traced lines. Place shapes, waxed side down, on wrong sides of selected fabrics. Use low heat and press to adhere to fabric. Cut out leaving roughly ¼" margin around paper shapes.

Step 3. Carefully press seam allowances to the back (freezer paper) side. Turn over and press lightly on the right side, correcting any areas that may not follow the shape smoothly. You may baste seam allowances in place if desired.

Step 4. From denim cut eight squares 3½" x 3½". Place one cat head and one dog muzzle/head each on a square. Insert appropriate ears as marked on pattern. Pin or baste pieces in place.

Step 5. With clear nylon monofilament in needle and neutral thread in bobbin, stitch around shapes with zigzag stitch. Catch base of ears when stitching around faces, but leave remainder of ears free.

Step 6. Cut denim away from behind each animal head, leaving ¼" around stitching, and remove freezer paper.

Step 7. Trace faces on cat and dog heads. With one strand of dark brown 6-strand embroidery floss, satin-stitch cat eye bottoms and noses. Stem-stitch the whiskers, tops of eyes, and area under nose. Satin-stitch dog eyes and noses with two strands of dark brown 6-strand embroidery floss. Stem-stitch under nose and work three French knots to each cheek with one strand of dark brown floss.

Step 8. Sew 3½" x 6½" rust plaid rectangles together alternately with appliquéd dog and cat squares with ¼" seam allowances to form a 72½" strip. Alternate dogs and cats, also. Sew remaining edges together to form a ring.

Step 9. Pin right side of appliqué strip to bottom edge of light side of skirt, cat ears pointing toward the waist. Sew with ¼" seam allowance.

Step 10. Sew piping to dark side of strip, raw edges aligned. Press appliquéd strip toward dark side of skirt. Whipstitch piping edge to skirt, taking care to pick up only one or two threads so stitches are not obvious on light side of skirt.

Step 11. Appliqué remaining cat to center front of remaining bodice (dark side).

Finishing

Step 1. Sew light bodice front and back together at sides.

Press seams open. Repeat with dark front and back.

Step 2. Layer bodices together, right sides facing. Sew tops of bodices together with ⅝" seam allowance. Leave bottom open. Turn right side out; press. Topstitch ¼" from edges.

Step 3. Sew gathering stitches at top of skirt. Pull gathers to fit bottom of bodice. Pin dark side of skirt to dark side of bodice, right sides facing; sew.

Step 4. Press raw edges of light bodice under ⅝". Whipstitch to light side of skirt, enclosing seams.

Step 5. Sew buttonholes on back shoulder straps. Sew buttons back to back on front shoulder strap. Place pink buttons on floral side and blue buttons on appliquéd side. ✂

**Country Jumper
Dog Face**

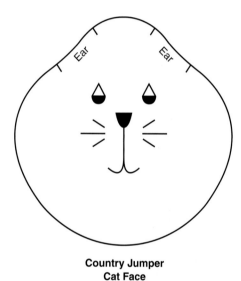

**Country Jumper
Cat Face**

**Country Jumper
Cat Ear**

**Country Jumper
Dog Muzzle**
Cut 4 medium tan

**Country Jumper
Dog Ear**

**Country Jumper
Dog Head**
Cut 4 dark tan

Button Bib Apron

By Holly Daniels

With a little imagination and a few more materials, you could make even more reversible bibs for this country apron.

Project Specifications

Skill Level: Beginner
Apron Size: Any size

Materials

- 1½ yards navy homespun plaid
- 8½" x 8½" squares each light and dark tan solid
- Scraps of 3 shades light tan for snowmen
- Scraps of green, red, blue and red-white-and-blue for appliqué
- 40" small cotton piping cord
- 5 (1") wooden buttons for waistband
- 7 (⅜"–⅝") assorted buttons for snowmen
- Scraps of fusible transfer web
- All-purpose threads to match fabrics
- Red, navy, light and dark tan machine-embroidery threads
- Dark brown, light tan, red, navy and orange 6-strand embroidery floss
- Tear-away fabric stabilizer
- Basic sewing supplies and tools

Instructions

Winter Bib

Step 1. Trace snowmen, mittens and muff on paper side of fusible transfer web as directed on pattern. Cut out leaving roughly ¼" around traced lines.

Step 2. Following manufacturer's instructions fuse appliqué shapes to selected fabrics. Cut out on traced lines.

Step 3. Referring to photo for placement, arrange snowmen along lower edge of 8½" x 8½" dark tan solid square. Fuse in place. Place tear-away fabric stabilizer behind appliqué area. Work machine-buttonhole or

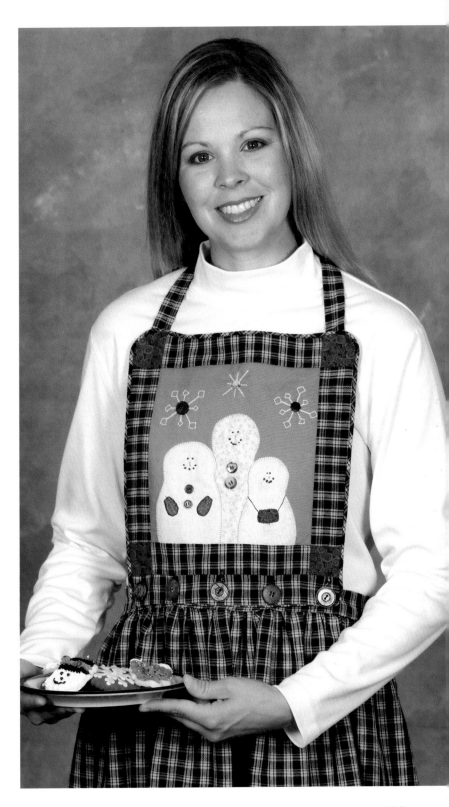

narrow zigzag stitch around shapes with dark tan machine-embroidery thread.

Step 4. Trace and stem-stitch muff cord with 3 strands of dark brown 6-strand embroidery floss.

Step 5. Referring to photo for placement, arrange mittens and muff on snowmen. Fuse and stitch as in Step 3.

Step 6. Transfer faces to snowmen. With 3 strands of dark brown 6-strand embroidery floss, make French knots for eyes and mouth. Use 3 strands of orange floss to embroider noses as shown in Fig. 1.

1. 2. 3.

Fig.1
Embroider snowman noses as shown.

Step 7. Referring to photo for placement, transfer snowflakes to background fabric and embroider all lines by hand or machine with light tan machine-embroidery thread or floss.

Step 8. Sew a button to the center of each snowflake and two buttons each to two snowmen referring to photo for placement. Remove fabric stabilizer from backside of piece.

Fourth of July Bib

Step 1. Trace firecrackers on paper side of fusible transfer web as directed on pattern. Cut out leaving roughly ¼" around traced lines. Referring to photo for placement, fuse and stitch as in Steps 2 and 3 above, using 8½" x 8½" light tan solid square and navy machine-embroidery thread.

Step 2. Trace the curved sparkle lines at the tops of the firecrackers on background fabric, reversing center sparkle line on red firecracker. Embroider all lines by hand or machine with red and navy threads or floss. Remove fabric stabilizer from backside of piece.

Bib Assembly

Step 1. From navy homespun plaid cut eight strips 2" x 8½". From red scraps cut eight 2" x 2" squares.

Step 2. Sew one navy homespun plaid strip to two opposite sides of each bib. Press seam allowances toward strips.

Step 3. Sew one red 2" x 2" square to each end of remaining navy homespun

plaid strips. Press seam allowances toward plaid. Sew one strip to top and bottom of each bib. Press seam allowances toward plaid strips.

Step 4. From navy homespun plaid cut two strips 2" x 11½". Sew one strip to bottom of each bib.

Step 5. Prepare 40" navy homespun plaid bias piping as shown on page 18. Place right sides of bibs together. Pin piping in place between bibs along top and side edges.

Step 6. From navy homespun plaid cut two strips 2½" x 27" for shoulder straps. Fold each in half lengthwise. Sew ¼" from raw edge on long side and one short side. Turn right side out; press. Insert between bib layers near upper outside edges, raw edges aligned. Pin in place.

Step 7. Starting at bib bottom, sew around bib leaving a 4" opening at lower edge for turning. Turn right side out; press. Close opening with hand stitches.

Apron Assembly

Step 1. From navy homespun plaid cut a 25" strip across the width of the fabric. Fold under ¼" on one long and both short sides; press. Fold under ¼" again and stitch for hem.

Step 2. From navy homespun plaid cut two strips 2½" x 25" for waist ties. Fold each in half lengthwise. Sew ¼" from raw edge on long side and one short side. Turn right side out; press.

Step 3. From navy homespun plaid cut two strips 2" x 21" for waistband. Press one long raw edge of one strip under ¼"; press. Place two long raw edges together, right sides facing. Sew with ¼" seam allowance.

Step 4. Gather top edge of apron skirt, by hand or machine, to 20" length. Place unpressed long edge of waistband and gathered skirt together, right sides facing. Pin skirt to waistband, leaving ½" free at each end. Stitch with ¼" seam allowance. Fold waistband over to other side and slipstitch folded edge to top of skirt, enclosing seam.

Step 5. Fold raw edges of waistband in

¼" on each side. Insert raw edge of one waist tie into each side of waistband about ½". Slipstitch or topstitch in place.

Step 6. Mark five buttonholes for 1" buttons evenly spaced across bottom of apron bib; stitch buttonholes. Center bib on waistband front. Mark button placement for five 1" wooden buttons and sew buttons to waistband to finish. ✄

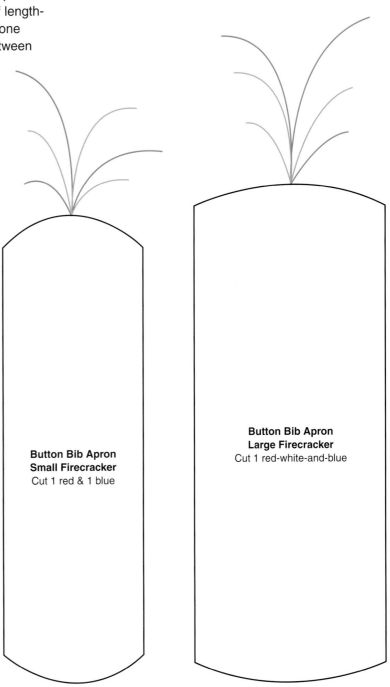

**Button Bib Apron
Small Firecracker**
Cut 1 red & 1 blue

**Button Bib Apron
Large Firecracker**
Cut 1 red-white-and-blue

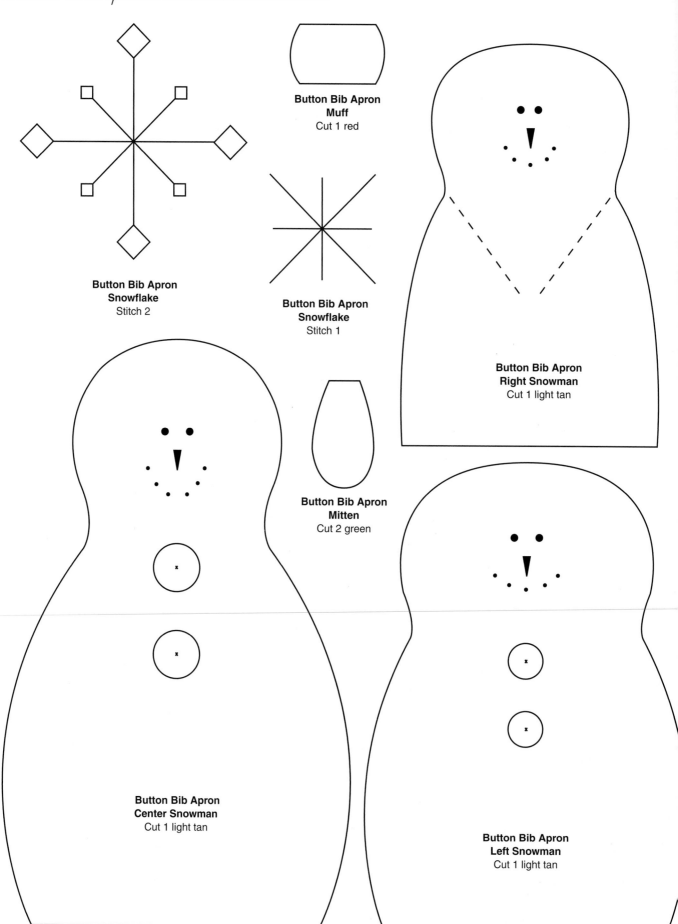

**Button Bib Apron
Muff**
Cut 1 red

**Button Bib Apron
Snowflake**
Stitch 2

**Button Bib Apron
Snowflake**
Stitch 1

**Button Bib Apron
Right Snowman**
Cut 1 light tan

**Button Bib Apron
Mitten**
Cut 2 green

**Button Bib Apron
Center Snowman**
Cut 1 light tan

**Button Bib Apron
Left Snowman**
Cut 1 light tan

Pillow Panels Trio

By Carol Zentgraf

Make a choice or sew three pillow styles—all reversible and all unique.

Project Specifications

Skill Level: Beginner

Flap Pillow Size: 14" x 14"

Buttoned Pillow: 12" x 18"

Mock Flange Pillow Size: 14" x 14" including flange and cord

Materials

For all Pillows

- All-purpose threads to match fabrics
- Basic sewing supplies

Flap Pillow

- 2 squares 14½" x 14½" medium floral decorator print for body of pillow
- 1 square each 14" x 14" coordinating large decorator floral print and plaid for flap
- 1 yard coordinating fringe
- ¼ yard coordinating narrow decorator cord for tie
- 14" x 14" pillow form

Buttoned Pillow

- 2 rectangles each 12" x 19" coordinating decorator print and plaid

- ¾ yard coordinating fringe with decorative header
- ¾ yard decorative coordinating braid
- 2 (1") matching or coordinating buttons
- 12" x 16" pillow form
- Permanent fabric adhesive

Mock Flange Pillow

- 2 squares each 15" x 15" medium floral decorator print and coordinating plaid for reversible panels
- 2 squares coordinating check 11" x 11" for pillow cover
- 3⅜ yards coordinating decorator cord with lip
- 2 yards narrow coordinating decorator cord for ties
- 10" x 10" pillow form

Instructions

***Note:** Use ½" seam allowances throughout.*

Flap Pillow

Step 1. Draw a triangle on each flap fabric that is 14" at the base and 12" high. Curve the side edges out as shown in Fig. 1. Cut one from each flap fabric.

Step 2. Referring to "Edge Finishes" on page 15, sew the curved flap sides together, sandwiching the bound

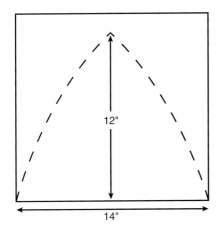

Fig. 1
Draw a triangle on each flap fabric that
is 14" at the base and 12" high. Curve
the side edges as shown.

edge of the coordinating fringe in the seam. Turn
the flap right side out and baste the 14" straight
edges together.

Step 3. Sew the two 14½" x 14½" pillow squares
together on three sides, right sides facing. Turn right
side out.

Step 4. With raw edges aligned, sew the flap to the
upper edge of one pillow panel. Insert the pillow form.
Press the seam toward the pillow. Press under ½" on
the edge of the remaining pillow panel and topstitch
the opening closed.

Step 5. Knot ends of narrow decorator cord. Measure 3"
from the flap tip and tie cord around the flap to gather.

Buttoned Pillow

Step 1. Following the instructions for "Edge Finishes"
on page 15, sew and assemble the two sets of 12" x
19" fabric rectangles.

Step 2. Topstitch both edges of the fringe header to
the pillow edge. On the reverse side, use permanent
fabric adhesive to adhere the decorative braid along
the edge.

Step 3. In the center of one side of panel make a 1"
buttonhole 1" from the fringe header.

Step 4. Sew one button on each side of the opposite panel. Insert pillow form and button the panel
edges together.

Mock Flange Pillow

Step 1. Right sides facing, sew the two 11" x 11"
fabric squares together, leaving an opening on side

to insert pillow form. Press edges under ½" on the
opening. Insert the pillow form and topstitch the
opening to close.

Step 2. Follow the instructions for "Edge Finishes"
on page 15 to sew one 15" square of each fabric
together with the coordinating decorator cord sandwiched between.

Step 3. At the center of each panel edge make a mark
1½" from the edge. Stitch a ½"-long buttonhole ¼" from
each side of each center mark as shown in Fig. 2.

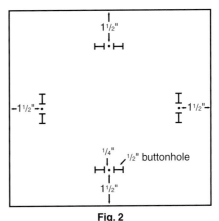

Fig. 2
Make a ½"-long buttonhole ¼" each
side of each center mark.

Step 4. Center the covered pillow form between the
two panels. Cut the narrow decorator cord in four
pieces. Lace one piece of cord through each set of
buttonholes to tie the panels together. Tie the cord into
bows on the pillow front. ✂

The Toile & Plaid Reversible Collection

By Pearl Louise Krush

This combination of bedroom accessories makes a total decorator ensemble. The reversibility of several items adds variety to the total look.

Project Specifications

Skill Level: Beginner

Duvet Cover Size: Double/Queen

Pillow Sham Size: Queen

Bed Skirt Size: Double/Queen with 12" drop

Table Cover Size: 24" x 26"

Table Topper Size: 43" x 43"

Lamp Shade Size: 4" x 11" x 7"

Curtain Panel Size: 44½" x 85½"

Valance Size: 15¼" x 65½"

Note: *Additional yardage may be necessary if matching prints or plaids or if bed, window or table sizes vary from model sizes.*

Materials

Duvet Cover
- 5 yards toile print
- 5 yards coordinating plaid
- 3 yards accent print for ruffle
- 2½ yards ¾"-wide hook-and-loop tape
- 7¾ yards ½"-wide gimp braid trim

Pillow Shams
- 1½ yards toile print
- 1½ yards coordinating plaid
- 1⅞ yards accent print for ruffle
- 6 yards ½"-wide gimp braid trim
- 1½ yards ¾"-wide hook-and-loop tape

Bed Skirt
- 5 yards muslin
- 3½ yards accent print for ruffle

Table Cover
- ¾ yard accent fabric for round top
- 2½ yards coordinating plaid for skirt
- Pattern-tracing paper

Table Topper
- 1 yard toile print
- 1 yard coordinating plaid
- 1⅜ yards accent print for ruffle
- 4⅛ yards ½"-wide gimp braid trim

Lamp Shade
- Self-adhesive lampshade 4" x 11" x 7"
- 3 yards ½"-wide gimp braid trim
- Cool-temperature glue gun and glue

Curtain Panels & Tiebacks
- 4⅞ yards toile print
- 4⅞ yards coordinating plaid
- ½ yard accent print for tiebacks
- 4 (1") plastic rings

Valance
- ¾ yard toile print
- ¾ yard coordinating plaid
- ¾ yard accent print
- 1⅔ yards ½"-wide gimp braid trim

All Projects
- All-purpose threads to match fabrics
- Basic sewing supplies and tools

Instructions

Duvet Cover

Note: *If matching prints or plaids adjust fabrics before cutting.*

Step 1. Cut toile print and coordinating plaid each into two 2½-yard lengths. Remove selvages.

Step 2. Sew the two matching lengths of each fabric together to make two different sides of duvet. Fold one end under 1½" on each duvet piece for closure end and stitch to hem.

Step 3. Remove selvages and cut 13 strips 8" wide across the width of the accent print. Sew strips together end to end for ruffle. Hem the two short ends of the ruffle strip. Fold in half lengthwise, wrong sides together;

press. Either machine-gather or hand-pleat the ruffle to fit around three sides of duvet (do not add ruffle to closure end).

Step 4. Align the raw edges of the ruffle with three outer edges of plaid side of the duvet. Stitch in place with ½" seam allowance.

Step 5. Place toile and plaid sides of duvet together, right sides facing, and sew around three sides. Do not stitch closure end. Turn right side out.

Step 6. Sew ½"-wide gimp braid trim around seam on toile side of duvet at the top of the ruffle.

Step 7. Cut hook-and-loop tape to fit across closure end of duvet. Separate strips of tape. Sew the loop side of tape to inside of toile hem. Sew hook side of tape to inside top edge of plaid hem.

Step 8. Insert comforter and press hook-and-loop strips together.

Bed Skirt

Step 1. Measure length of box springs. Cut two muslin strips that length. Sew two lengths together on long edge. Press seam open. Remove excess fabric to fit width of box springs. Press under ¼" on one short edge. Press under another ½" and stitch to hem.

Step 2. Remove selvages from accent print. Cut nine 13¼"-wide strips across width of fabric for ruffle. Sew strips together end to end. Sew narrow hems on each short end.

Step 3. Press under ¼" on one long edge. Press under another ½" and stitch to hem.

Step 4. Either machine-gather or hand-pleat the ruffle to fit around two sides and unhemmed end of muslin. Align raw edges and stitch with ½" seam allowance on three sides.

Pillow Shams

Step 1. Cut two pieces each 24" x 28" from toile print and coordinating plaid. Remove selvages and cut eight 8"-wide strips across the width of accent fabric for ruffles.

Step 2. Press under ½" and then 1" on one short end of each rectangle for hem.

Step 3. Sew four ruffle strips together end to end for each sham. Sew ends of each strip together to make a ring. Bring raw edges of each ring together, wrong sides facing; press. Either machine-gather or hand-pleat the ruffle to fit around all four edges of plaid rectangle. Align raw edges and stitch with ¼" seam allowance on three sides. On hemmed edge, stitch ruffle to rectangle along previously stitched hem seam.

Step 4. Place toile print rectangle on top of plaid, matching hemmed ends, right sides facing. Stitch around three edges on previous stitching line. Hand-stitch the backside of the ruffle on the open end of the sham to the top of the hemmed edge to cover raw edges.

Step 5. Add ½"-wide gimp braid trim and hook-and-loop tape to openings as in Steps 6 and 7 of Duvet Cover.

Step 6. Insert pillows and close with hook-and-loop strips.

Curtain Panels & Tiebacks

Step 1. Remove selvages and cut two 86" x 45" panels each from toile print and coordinating plaid.

Step 2. Place a toile print and a plaid panel together, right sides facing, and sew around perimeter with ¼" seam allowance leaving a 6" opening for turning. Turn right side out and close opening with hand stitches. Repeat for second panel.

Step 3. Sew a line across the width of each panel 2" down from the top edge. Sew another line 2" down from the first to make a casing in each panel.

Step 4. Remove the stitches between the casing lines at the outer edges of each panel. Hand-stitch the seam allowance under at each side.

Step 5. Cut two strips 8" x 30" from accent print. Fold each in half lengthwise, right sides facing. Sew each strip on long edge with ¼" seam allowance. Turn right side out; press.

Step 6. Turn short ends in on each strip and topstitch. Sew a 1" plastic ring to the center of each short end of each strip.

Valance

Step 1. Cut one 12" x 42" and one 12" x 24" strip each from toile print and coordinating plaid. Sew 12" ends of matching fabrics together to make one long strip of each.

Step 2. Remove selvages and cut three 8"-wide strips across the width of accent print. Sew strips end to end. Fold in half lengthwise; press.

Step 3. Either machine-gather or hand-pleat the raw edges to fit the bottom edge of valance strip. Align raw edges and sew ruffle strip to toile valance strip with ¼" seam allowance. Place plaid valance strip on toile strip, right sides facing. Sew around perimeter with ¼" seam allowance, leaving an 8" opening for turning. Turn right side out and close opening with hand stitches.

Step 4. Sew a line across the width of the valance 3" down from the top edge. Sew another line 3" down from the first to make a casing. Remove the stitches between the casing lines at the outer edges of valance. Hand-stitch the seam allowance under at each side.

Table Topper

Step 1. Cut one 36" x 36" square each from toile print and coordinating plaid.

Step 2. Remove selvages and cut six 8"-wide strips across the width of accent print. Sew strips together end to end to form a ring. Bring raw edges together, wrong sides facing; press.

Step 3. Either machine-gather or hand-pleat the raw edges to fit around the 36" x 36" plaid square. Align raw edges of ruffle with raw edges of square and stitch in place with ¼" seam allowance.

Step 4. Place the two 36" fabric squares together, right sides facing, and stitch around the perimeter,

leaving an 8" opening in one side for turning. Turn right side out and close opening with hand stitches.

Step 5. Sew ½"-wide gimp braid trim around all four edges at top of ruffle.

Table Cover

Step 1. Trace table-top circle on pattern paper. Add ¼" seam allowance. Trace circle on accent fabric and cut out.

Step 2. Measure desired drop and add ¾". Cut two lengths of coordinating plaid that length across the width of fabric. Remove selvages. Seam the two fabric panels together on selvage edges to form a ring.

Step 3. Press under ¼", then ¼" again on one raw edge. Stitch for hem. Either machine-gather or hand-pleat the other raw edge to fit the circle. Right sides facing, stitch gathered plaid to round circle. Place on table.

Lamp Shade

Step 1. Peel off the outer cover of lamp shade to use for pattern. Place on accent print fabric. Add ½" on all edges and cut out.

Step 2. Carefully press fabric onto sticky shade. Fold and overlap the ends. Glue the folded side in place with cool-temperature glue gun.

Step 3. Clip the outer curved fabric edges at the top and bottom of shade. Fold to the inside.

Step 4. Glue the ½"-wide gimp braid trim to the inside and the outside of the top and bottom shade edges to finish. ✄

Floral Plaid Ensemble

By Carol Zentgraf

This window treatment and chair cushion have a very expensive custom look
that you will be able to complete with ease and great satisfaction.

Project Specifications

Skill Level: Beginner

Rod Size: Any size

Valance Size: Any size

Cushion Size: Any size

Note: *Model valance fits window 44" wide and 40" long, including frame. Adjust yardage for other window sizes.*

Materials

- 4½ yards each coordinating print and plaid 54"-wide decorator fabrics
- Length of PVC pipe or upholstery fabric cardboard bolt 13" longer than width of window in diameter of your choice
- 2 (1½") buttons
- 2 tennis balls
- 5 yards cotton upholsterer's cord
- ½ yard heavy twisted decorative cord for ends of rod
- 1¼ yards narrow twisted cord to tie rosettes
- 2 yards ⅛"-wide satin ribbon for chair ties
- 2 chair-seat size batting squares
- Batting the length of rod by the circumference of rod
- All-purpose sewing threads to match fabrics
- Hot-glue gun and glue
- 2 rubber bands
- Transparent packing tape
- Pattern-tracing cloth
- Basic sewing supplies and tools

Instructions

Note: *Use ½" seam allowances throughout.*

Cushion

Step 1. Draw outline of chair seat on pattern-tracing cloth. Cut two layers of batting and one layer of each fabric.

Step 2. Determine desired ruffle depth (drop). Double the depth and add 1" for seam allowance to obtain cutting width of ruffle.

Step 3. Measure each side and the front of cushion. Double each of the three measurements and cut one strip each by the cutting width of the ruffle.

Step 4. Sew one short end of each side strip to short ends of front strip. Press the seams open. Fold strip in half lengthwise, wrong sides together. Press the fold and baste the raw edges together.

Step 5. With raw edges aligned, pin ruffle strip to right side of one cushion panel, matching front corners and back corners. Hand-pleat, pinning in place around the edges.

Step 6. Cut ⅛"-wide satin ribbon in four pieces. Pin two lengths to each back corner of cushion for ties. Baste the ruffle and ties to cushion.

Step 7. Layer cushion pieces right sides facing and

with two layers of batting on top. Stitch around perimeter, leaving an opening in back for turning. Turn right side out and close opening with hand stitches.

Valance

Step 1. To determine valance panel measurements, measure window and frame to determine valance width and drop needed. Add 1" to each measurement for seam allowances.

Step 2. From each fabric cut one 40" panel in the determined valance width dimension, cutting across the fabric width. Cut two 40" panels in the determined drop length from each fabric, cutting across the fabric width.

Step 3. For each fabric, sew a drop panel to each end of valance panel. Press the seams open and fold each panel in half, bringing short ends together, right sides facing.

Step 4. Place a folded panel on a large work surface. To measure and cut the jabot angle, divide your window width by two, then add 10" to that figure. Measure that total from the fold and mark the lower edge of the fabric. Draw a line from the lower edge mark to the upper outside corner as shown in Fig. 1. Cut on this line. Repeat on other panel.

Step 5. Refer to the instructions on page 17 to cut continuous binding and to cover and apply upholsterer's cord. Sew the two fabric panels together with the cord along the angled and lower edges.

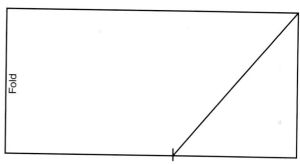

Fig.1
Draw a line from marked lower edge to upper outside corner.

Rosettes

Step 1. To make rosettes cut two 22"-diameter fabric circles. Sew a gathering stitch 6" from the outer edge and another gathering stitch along the outer edge. Pull the inner gathering threads to gather, and knot the ends of the thread.

Step 2. Gather the outer edges and knot the ends of the thread. Bring the gathered edges together to form a ro-sette. Hand-stitch the edges together as shown in Fig. 2.

Fig. 2
Bring gathered edges together and hand-stitch.

Step 3. Sew or glue a button to the center of each gathered rosette.

Step 4. Cut the twisted decorative cord in half. Hand-tack the center of each length to the backside of a rosette.

Rod

Step 1. Hot-glue batting to rod.

Step 2. Cut fabric the length of rod plus 1" and circumference of rod plus 1". Wrap rod with fabric, folding one long edge under ½" and overlapping the other long edge. Tuck short ends into ends of rod. Hot-glue in place.

Step 3. For finials, cut two 14" circles of fabric. Wrap one fabric circle around each tennis ball, securing with

rubber band. Wrap gathered ends tightly with transparent packing tape as shown in Fig. 3. Insert taped end of each ball into ends of rod. Hot-glue finials to rod.

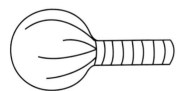

Fig. 3
Wrap gathered fabric tightly with transparent packing tape.

Step 4. Cut two lengths of heavy twisted decorative cord the circumference of rod. Hot-glue around the end of each rod to cover seam between rod and finial.

Step 5. Fold valance in deep folds as shown in Fig. 4. Tie ends of rosette cords at each end of valance panel, then tie valance to rod with ends of rosette cords. ✂

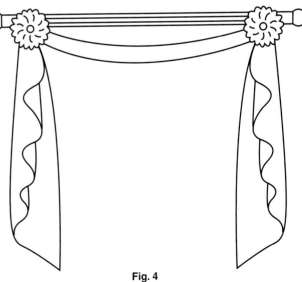

Fig. 4
Fold valance in deep folds and tie to rod with rosette cords.

Birdhouse/Gingerbread Swag

By Holly Daniels

Decorate your holiday home with gingerbread houses, and the rest of the year flip to the reverse for cheerful birdhouses—double-duty decor!

Project Specifications

Skill Level: Beginner

Swag Size: Approximately 46" x 5½"

Materials

- 3 squares brown print 6¾" x 6¾"
- 1 square each 6¾" x 6¾" blue, tan and yellow prints
- Scraps of blue, yellow, brown and red for appliqué and roofs
- Buttons in assorted styles and sizes
- Scraps of assorted trims (rickrack, ribbon, 6-strand embroidery floss, etc.)
- Scraps of fusible transfer web
- Scraps of thin batting
- Scraps of fabric stabilizer
- All-purpose threads to match and contrast with fabrics
- 5 yards of twine
- 3 large eyes from hook-and-eye sets
- Basic sewing supplies and tools

Instructions

Step 1. Cut house shapes as directed on pattern.

Step 2. Trace gingerbread door and window shapes and birdhouse entry holes on paper side of fusible transfer web. Cut out leaving roughly ¼" margin around traced shapes. Following manufacturer's directions, fuse to selected fabrics. Refer to photo for ideas. Cut out on traced lines.

Step 3. Referring to photo, position appliqué pieces on houses; fuse. Pin fabric stabilizer on backside of appliqués. Machine-appliqué around each shape with satin or buttonhole stitch. Remove stabilizer.

Step 4. Machine-stitch a ¼" circle under birdhouse entry to represent a perch. Sew a small button to each gingerbread house door for a doorknob.

Step 5. Two house roof patterns are included. Select a roof style and fabric for each house shape and cut two

of each. Place two matching roof shapes together, right sides facing. Stitch on curved edges only with ¼" seam allowance. Clip curves and notches. Turn right side out; press. Align straight edges of roof shapes with straight top edges of houses. Baste along straight edges, leaving previously stitched curved edges loose.

Step 6. For gingerbread house variations, try some decorative machine stitches or hand-embroider details. Refer to photo for ideas. Flowers can be created using buttons for blossoms. Embroider the stems. Tiny crossed candy canes are embroidered in red stem stitch and couched with white. Silk flowers and bows may be added.

Step 7. Add birdhouse variations with rickrack, strips of fabric, decorative stitches, buttons, etc.

Step 8. Place birdhouse batting shapes on work surface. Place a birdhouse right side up on batting and a gingerbread house right side down. Sew around perimeter with ¼" seam allowance, leaving opening at bottom for turning. Trim seam allowances and turn right side out; press. Close opening with hand stitches. Repeat for three reversible house units.

Step 9. Trace and cut hearts as directed on pattern. Place batting on work surface. Top with one blue heart right side up and a red heart right side down. Sew around perimeter with ¼" seam allowance. Leave an

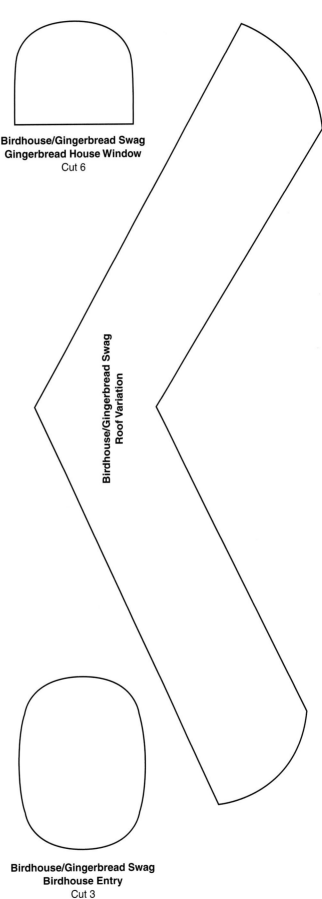

**Birdhouse/Gingerbread Swag
Gingerbread House Window**
Cut 6

**Birdhouse/Gingerbread Swag
Roof Variation**

**Birdhouse/Gingerbread Swag
Birdhouse Entry**
Cut 3

Birdhouse/Gingerbread Swag
Gingerbread House
Cut 3 brown, 1 tan, 1 yellow & 1 blue
Cut 3 batting

Birdhouse/Gingerbread Swag Gingerbread House Door
Cut 3

Birdhouse/Gingerbread Swag Roof

opening for turning. Clip curves and notches and trim seam allowances. Turn right side out and close openings with hand stitches. Make two reversible heart units.

Step 10. Sew a button to center of each blue heart. Cut two 8" pieces of twine. Tie each into a tight bow. Cut two 20" pieces of twine. Sew the center of each 20" twine to the center of a red heart right behind the button. Hand-tack a bow on top of stitched twine.

Step 11. Cut three 36" pieces of twine. Tie a tight bow in the center of each piece and tack bow to gingerbread house as shown in photo. Allow twine to curve down slightly and tack in place where house meets roof. Repeat for each gingerbread house.

Step 12. Sew the eye portion of hook-and-eye sets to peak of each roof for a hanger. A plastic ring or hand-worked button loop could be substituted, if desired.

Step 13. Tie ends of twine between houses and hearts into bows. Tie so that bows are approximately 3" from edges of houses and hearts. Trim ends of twine. ✂

Birdhouse/Gingerbread Swag Heart
Cut 2 red, 2 blue & 2 batting

Festive Table Mat

By Marian Shenk

This lovely piece is planned to grace your table year-round—one side or the other.

Project Specifications

Skill Level: Beginner
Table Mat Size: Approximately 25" in diameter

Materials

- ½ yard multicolored red-green-blue-and-metallic gold print
- ¼ yard each red and blue coordinating prints
- ¾ yard white-on-white print
- Lavender, peach, light green, yellow, blue, pink, dark green and gold print scraps for appliqué
- 1 yard fusible transfer web
- Compass
- Pattern paper
- ⅞ yard ⅜"-wide gold metallic trim
- 8 yards ⅛"-wide gold metallic trim
- Gold metallic thread
- Machine-appliqué threads to match appliqués
- All-purpose threads to match fabrics
- Basic sewing supplies and tools

Instructions

Stained Glass Mat

Step 1. Trace and cut stained glass pieces as directed on patterns A, B and C.

Step 2. Sew one multicolored print A to a red or blue A for a total of 12 units as shown in Fig. 1. Sew one red B to each blue unit and one blue B to each red unit as shown in Fig. 2.

Step 3. Join all units in a circle as shown in Fig. 3. Appliqué C to center of circle.

Step 4. With gold metallic thread and zigzag stitch, sew ⅛"-wide metallic trim over all seams. Start with outside to center straight seams, then angled and center circle as shown in photo; press.

Spring Flower Mat

Step 1. Trace and cut pieces as directed on pattern D. Draw a 9½"-diameter circle on pattern paper with compass. Use this pattern to cut one white-on-white center circle.

Step 2. Sew all D pieces together in a circle as shown in Fig. 4. Appliqué the center circle in place.

Step 3. Trace appliqué shapes E, F and G on paper side of fusible transfer web. Cut out leaving roughly ¼" margin around traced lines. Following manufacturer's instructions, fuse to selected fabrics. Cut out on traced lines.

Step 4. Referring to photo for placement, arrange flowers and leaves on mat; fuse.

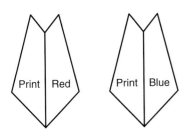

Fig. 1
Join A pieces as shown for a total of
6 red units and 6 blue units.

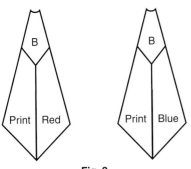

Fig. 2
Sew a red B to blue units and blue B to
red units.

Step 5. Draw stems on leaves
and flowers.

Step 6. With matching machine-embroidery threads
work satin stitch around all appliqués. With green
thread work satin stitch over marked stems.

Step 7. With gold metallic thread and zigzag stitch sew
⅜"-wide gold metallic trim over center circle seam.

Step 8. Place two mats right sides together and sew
around perimeter, leaving opening for turning. Clip
inside corners and outside points.

Step 9. Turn mat right side out and close opening with
hand stitches. ✂

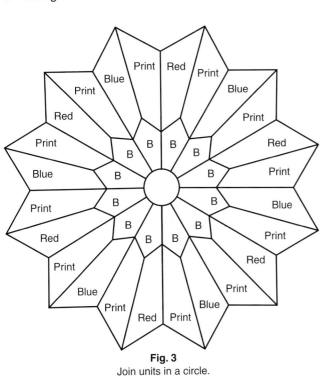

Fig. 3
Join units in a circle.

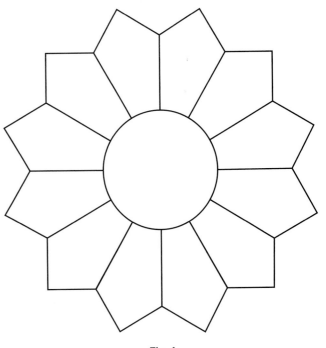

Fig. 4
Sew D units together in a circle.

Festive Table Mat
Spring Flower
E
Cut 2 peach, 2 lavender, 2 light green,
2 yellow, 2 blue & 2 pink

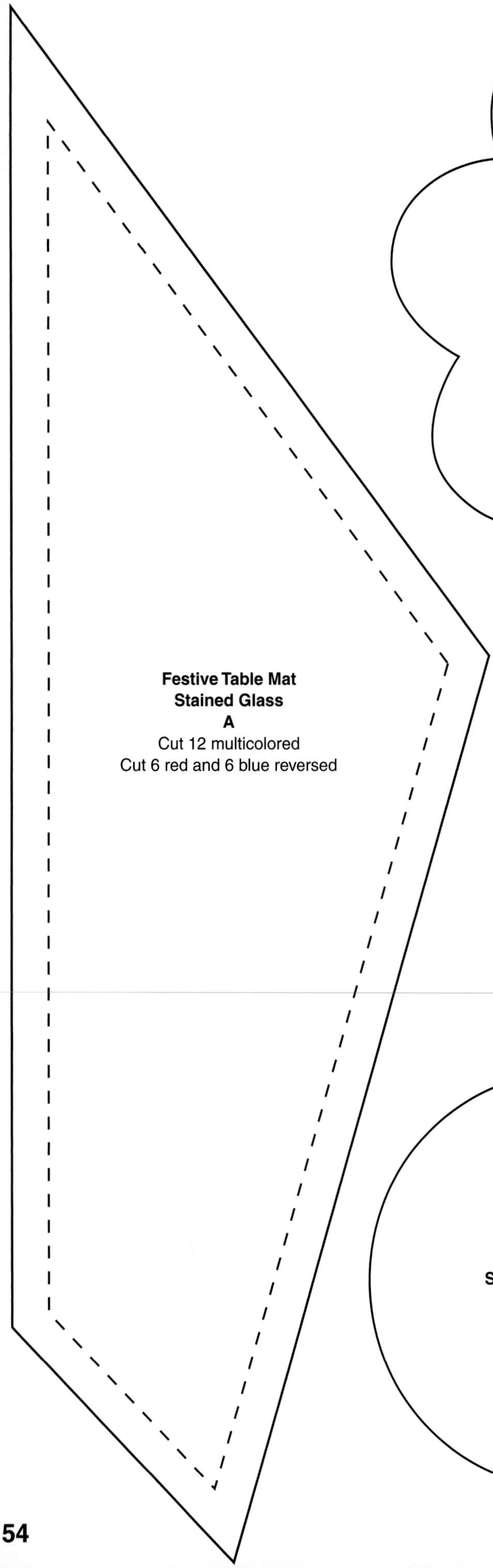

Festive Table Mat
Stained Glass
A
Cut 12 multicolored
Cut 6 red and 6 blue reversed

Festive Table Mat
Stained Glass
B
Cut 6 red & 6 blue

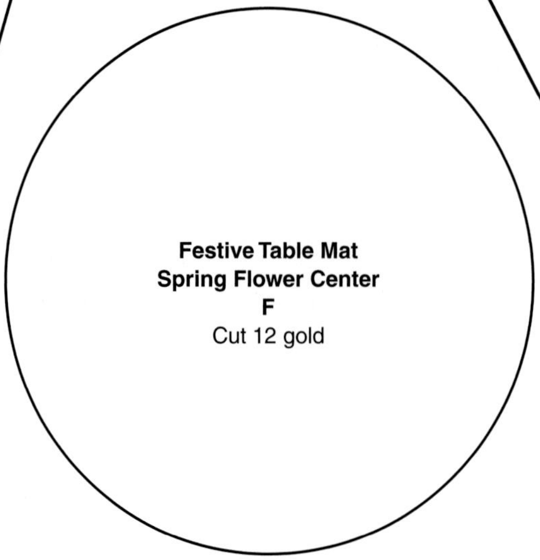

Festive Table Mat
Spring Flower Center
F
Cut 12 gold

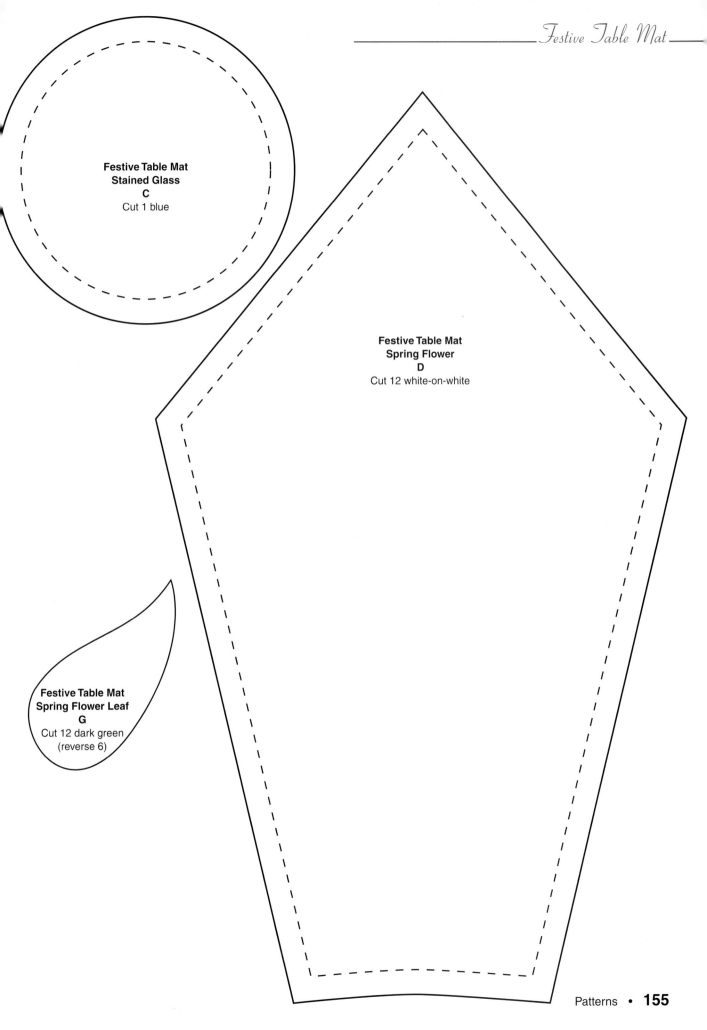

**Festive Table Mat
Stained Glass
C**
Cut 1 blue

**Festive Table Mat
Spring Flower
D**
Cut 12 white-on-white

**Festive Table Mat
Spring Flower Leaf
G**
Cut 12 dark green
(reverse 6)

Foundation-Pieced Table Runner

By Carol Zentgraf

Create an everyday table runner that reverses for a special-occasion accent. It's easy with double-layer foundation piecing!

Project Specifications

Skill Level: Beginner

Table Runner Size: 36" x 18"

Note: *Pattern and yardage can be easily adjusted for other sizes.*

Materials

- ½ yard pieces of 4–6 coordinating prints for each side
- 18" x 36" muslin for foundation
- 3¼ yards purchased or self-made bias binding
- Pattern-tracing cloth
- Rotary-cutting tools
- All-purpose threads to match fabrics

- Basic sewing supplies and tools

Instructions

Note: *Use ¼" seam allowances throughout.*

Step 1. Referring to Fig. 1, mark and draw lines on muslin foundation. Create templates, cut fabrics and piece runner referring to "Double-Layer Foundation Piecing" on page 63.

Step 2. Trim piece to 18" x 36". Curve corners using plate or other curved object as a guide.

Step 3. Bind edges with purchased or self-made bias binding.

Step 4. Seam lines may be embellished with ribbons, trims or decorative stitches. ✂

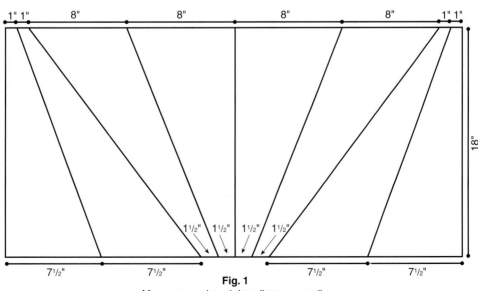

Fig. 1
Measure, mark and draw lines on muslin
foundation as shown.

Changeable Flap Handbag

By Carol Zentgraf

It's a snap to change the look of this reversible bag with a variety of coordinating flaps.

Project Specifications

Skill Level: Beginner

Handbag Size: Any size

Materials

- Commercial pattern for lined handbag with strap
- ½ yard each of two quilted or heavy cotton fabrics for bag base
- ¼ yard contrasting or matching fabrics for each side of each flap
- ½ yard medium-weight fusible interfacing
- Decorative snaps in colors of your choice
- Snap-setting tool
- Pattern-tracing cloth
- Contrasting or matching all-purpose threads
- Basic sewing supplies and tools

Instructions

Note: *Use ⅝" seam allowance throughout.*

Step 1. If handbag back and flap are one continuous pattern piece, pattern will need to be revised. Place front pattern on back pattern, aligning side and lower edges. Cut back pattern even with front upper edge. Use pattern-tracing cloth to add 1⅝" to the flap cut edge for an overlap as shown in Fig. 1.

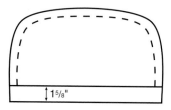

Fig. 1
Use pattern-tracing cloth to add 1⅝"
to flap edge.

Step 2. From each base fabric cut one each of the front, back, strap and side/bottom gusset. Using adjusted flap pattern, cut one flap each from four selected flap fabrics. Cut two flap pieces from fusible interfacing.

Step 3. Following manufacturer's instructions, fuse interfacing to wrong side of two fabric flaps. Right sides facing, sew an interfaced flap to each remaining flap, leaving an opening in flat edge for turning. Trim seams and curves and turn right side out. Press seam allow-ances of opening under and topstitch straight edge.

Step 4. Follow pattern guide sheet to construct lined handbag base and strap.

Step 5. Place the topstitched edge of one flap along the upper edge of the handbag back, overlapping 1" as shown in Fig. 2. Mark a snap placement at each end of the flap and one in the center. The center of the snap should be ½" from the topstitched edge.

Step 6. Follow the manufacturer's instructions to apply a snap cap at each position on the flap. Reposition the flap on the handbag and

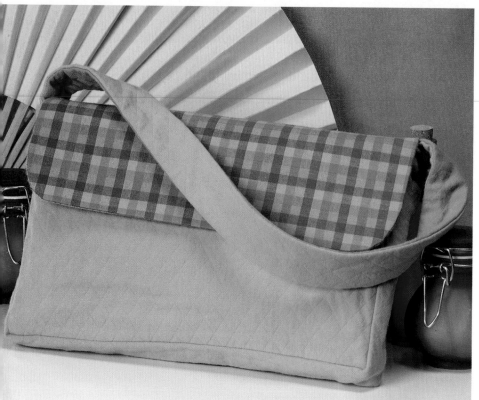

mark the corresponding snap base placements. Apply the bases on the handbag.

Step 7. Turn the flap over and mark a snap placement ¾" on each side of the center snap and ¾" from each end snap. Apply the snap caps.

Step 8. Reverse the handbag to its other side. Mark and apply the snap bases to the upper edge of this side as shown in Fig. 3.

Step 9. Apply snap caps to the remaining flap to correspond with the first flap. ✂

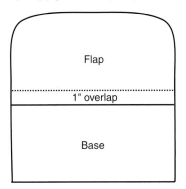

Fig. 2
Place topstitched edge of flap along
upper edge of handbag back as shown.

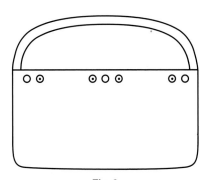

Fig. 3
Apply snap bases as shown.

Tapestry Safari Vest

By Carol Zentgraf

Discover the fun of working with tapestry fabrics. The reverse side of any design will be a subtle reflection of your choice.

Project Specifications

Skill Level: Beginner
Vest Size: Any size

Materials

- Unlined commercial vest pattern
- Tapestry fabric in yardage indicated on pattern. Allow extra if motifs are to be centered
- 2 packages coordinating double-fold bias tape
- Frog closure or cord to make frog
- Matching and contrasting all-purpose threads
- ¼"-wide fusible basting tape
- Permanent fabric adhesive (optional)
- Basic sewing supplies and tools

Instructions

Note: *Use a ⅝" seam allowance and sew seams right sides facing.*

Step 1. Cut vest fronts and back from tapestry fabric following pattern guide sheet. Eliminate facings and center overlap. If using scenic fabric as featured in model, center the pattern pieces over the desired motifs before cutting.

Step 2. Sew vest fronts to back at shoulders and side seams. Press seams open.

Step 3. Working with one seam allowance at a time on fabrics that fray easily, follow the instructions for bound seam allowances and edges on pages 31–34 in "Reversible Single-Layer Sewing." Use ¼"-wide fusible basting tape to secure the bias tape in place. Bind shoulder and side seam allowances. Topstitch the seam allowances to the vest.

Step 4. Trim the seam allowances and bind the armhole and outer edges of the vest.

Step 5. Follow the instructions for frog closures on page 48 or use a purchased frog closure. Place vest on work surface with center edges just meeting. Position frog halves on the vest front and stitch in place or secure with permanent fabric adhesive. ✂

Double-Layer Suede Vest

By Carol Zentgraf

*Create a faux suede vest with two distinctly different layers
that share a common decorative-edge treatment.*

Project Specifications

Skill Level: Beginner

Vest Size: Any size

Materials

- Commercial vest pattern
- Two different colors of Ultrasuede Light™, each in yardage indicated on pattern for one vest

- Rotary cutter with decorative pinking blade
- Rotary-cutting mat
- Rubber leaf stamp
- Red, green and gold fabric paints
- Size #8 flat paintbrush
- 1 (1¾") decorative button
- 1 (2¼") wooden toggle button
- All-purpose threads that match fabrics
- Basic sewing supplies and tools

Instructions

Note: *Use ⅝" seam allowance. Refer to "Specialty Fabrics" on page 40 for sewing faux suede fabric.*

Step 1. Follow pattern guide sheet to cut vest fronts and back from each fabric. Use nap layout.

Step 2. Sew each set of fronts to corresponding back of vest at shoulder and side seams. Press the seams open.

Step 3. Place vest to be stamped on flat work surface and overlap front edges. Plan the stamping design. Mark button and loop closure placement.

Step 4. Refer to "Stamping" on page 56 and stamp the leaf design on the vest fronts. Allow paint to dry thoroughly.

Step 5. Following the instructions for "Wrong Sides Facing Assembly" on page 23, stitch the vests together along all raw edges. Trim edges near stitching line with rotary cutter pinking blade.

Step 6. Sew 1¾" button at placement mark on one side of vest and 2¼" wooden toggle on the reverse side. Be sure to sew through only one layer of vest on each side.

Step 7. For each button loop cut a ½" x 20" strip of Ultrasuede Light™. Fold each strip in half lengthwise and stitch close to raw edges. Make a loop large enough to go around the button, then machine-tack the loop to the vest front at the placement mark, letting the loose ends hang free. The machine stitching on each side will be covered by the overlap when worn. ✀

Frayed Edges Vest

By Carol Zentgraf

Red faux chenille adds zip to one side of this vest, which reverses to a more conservative design.

Project Specifications

Skill Level: Beginner

Vest Size: Any size

Materials

- Commercial unlined vest with no-button front
- Denim or sturdy cotton fabric in yardage indicated on pattern
- 1 package red chenille trim
- Chenille brush
- 3 yards of ⅜"-wide braid or trim
- Matching and contrasting all-purpose threads
- Dressmaker's chalk
- Permanent fabric adhesive
- Basic sewing supplies and tools

Instructions

Note: *Use ⅝" seam allowance throughout.*

Step 1. Cut vest fronts and back using pattern guide sheet. Eliminate facings.

Step 2. Sew vest fronts to back at shoulders and sides.

Step 3. Press seams open. Topstitch the seams in place, stitching ¼" on each side of seam line.

Step 4. Use contrasting thread and zigzag-stitch ⅝" from all raw edges. See "Fray Frenzy" on page 27 and follow directions to fray all seam and raw edges up to the stitching lines.

Step 5. Place vest on flat work surface. Referring to the photo, use dressmaker's chalk to sketch an embellishment design on the vest fronts.

Step 6. Follow manufacturer's instructions to stitch chenille trim to the design lines. Spray the trim with water and brush with the chenille brush until the strips are frayed.

Step 7. On the reverse side of vest apply ⅜"-wide braid or trim to front and neckline edges. Position ¼" from contrasting zigzag stitch line. Adhere with permanent fabric adhesive. ✂

Suede Shirt Jacket

By Carol Zentgraf

*Decorative seam allowances and punched facings make
this jacket completely reversible with a minimum of finishing fuss.*

Project Specifications

Skill Level: Beginner
Shirt Jacket Size: Any size

Materials

- Commercial shirt jacket pattern
- Ultrasuede Soft™ in yardage indicated on pattern
- Fusible interfacing and notions indicated on pattern
- Twice the number of buttons required on pattern
- Rotary cutter with decorative wave blade
- Rotary-cutting mat
- Round and teardrop leather punches, mat and mallet
- Transparent tear-away fabric stabilizer
- All-purpose thread to match fabric
- Basic sewing supplies and tools

Instructions

Note: *Use a ⅝" seam allowance and sew seams right sides facing. Refer to "Specialty Fabrics" on page 40 for sewing faux suede fabric.*

Step 1. Use nap layout and cut pattern pieces following pattern guide sheet.

Step 2. Fuse interfacing to facings and under collar pieces following manufacturer's directions.

Step 3. To embellish facing, trim the outer edges with the rotary cutter and decorative wave blade. Use the leather punches, mat and mallet to punch a design along the trimmed edges as shown in Fig. 1.

Fig. 1
Punch a design along edges of facings as shown.

Step 4. Punch random motifs over entire facing pieces as shown in Fig. 2.

Step 5. Follow the pattern guide sheet to assemble the jacket, eliminating hemming steps for the hemline and cuffs. Use fabric stabilizer when making buttonholes. Wrap stabilizer around collar edge and front edges before topstitching. Remove stabilizer when stitching is complete.

Step 6. Sew buttons onto each side of left front to correspond with buttonholes.

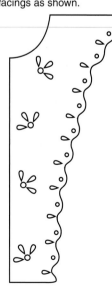

Fig. 2
Punch random motifs over entire facing as shown.

Fig. 3
Punch hemlines and cuffs with design as shown.

Step 7. Use rotary cutter with decorative wave blade to trim the hemline and cuffs. Embellish the edges with a punched design as shown in Fig. 3. ✂

Fleece Patch Pocket Jacket

By Carol Zentgraf

If you reverse this jacket—welt pockets are featured! And although still worn buttoned on the reverse side, the edges appear to be plain.

Project Specifications

Skill Level: Beginner
Jacket Size: Any size

Materials

- Commercial fleece jacket pattern featuring patch pockets
- Fleece in yardage indicated on pattern
- 1 package of precut Lycra™ binding in 2" or 2½" width
- 4 (¾") buttons
- Matching and contrasting all-purpose threads
- ¼"-wide self-adhesive basting tape
- Tear-away fabric stabilizer
- Basic sewing supplies and tools

Instructions

Step 1. Follow the pattern guide sheet to cut jacket pieces from fleece fabric.

Step 2. Refer to "Fleece" instructions on page 42, "Pockets" on pages 36–38 and "Mock Flat-Felled Seams" on page 35.

Step 3. Cut two welts equal in width to the pocket upper edge. On each jacket front, apply the welt and slit, then apply the patch pocket to the reverse side. Use the ¼"-wide self-adhesive basting tape to secure the pockets as you work.

Step 4. Construct the jacket following the pattern guide sheet. Finish all seams except the underarm sleeve seam with a topstitched or zigzag mock flat-felled finish. Trim the sleeve seam close to the stitching.

Step 5. Bind the sleeve and outer edges with 2" or 2½" precut Lycra™ binding.

Step 6. Stitch four ¾" buttonholes, using tear-away fabric stabilizer on both sides of the fleece. Sew buttons in place to match button-hole positions. ✀

Outline-Stitched Jacket

By Carol Zentgraf

Not only do you get double-design with this jacket, but snuggly double-layer warmth!

Project Specifications

Skill Level: Beginner
Jaclet Size: Any size

Materials

- Reversible jacket pattern designed for fleece
- Solid and print fleece fabrics in yardage indicated on pattern
- 6 (⅞") buttons
- Transparent water-soluble fabric stabilizer
- All-purpose threads to match fabrics
- Machine-quilting thread in color that contrasts with solid fabric
- Basic sewing supplies and tools

Instructions

Note: *Use ⅝" seam allowances throughout. Refer to "Specialty Fabrics" on page 40 for sewing fleece fabrics.*

Step 1. Follow the pattern guide sheet to cut out the pattern pieces and construct the jacket as instructed. Make buttonholes and sew on buttons.

Step 2. On the print side of the jacket select the pattern motifs that you would like to outline-stitch. Consider their placement on the solid reverse side of the jacket.

Step 3. Pin the transparent water-soluble fabric stabilizer over the motifs to be stitched. Trace the motifs onto the stabilizer.

Step 4. Use quilting thread in both needle and bobbin and lengthen machine stitch length to 5.0 or 5.5. With the print side up, stitch along the traced lines, being careful not to twist or distort the fleece layers. Remove the stabilizer. ✂

Color-Block Melton Jacket

By Carol Zentgraf

Melton and other coat-weight non-fraying wool fabrics maintain their shape and don't ravel when cut in shapes or at angles.

Project Specifications

Skill Level: Beginner

Jacket Size: Any size

Materials

- Commercial jacket or coat pattern designed for single-layer sewing
- Melton or coat-weight wool in yardage indicated on pattern
- 2 (1⅛") buttons

- Transparent tear-away fabric stabilizer
- Pattern-tracing cloth
- Rotary cutter with decorative blades
- Rotary-cutting mat
- Clear acrylic quilter's ruler
- All-purpose threads to match fabric
- Permanent fabric adhesive (optional)
- Basic sewing supplies and tools

Instructions

Note: *The featured jacket was color-blocked on the collar, cuffs and pockets. You can also color-block the front edges or hemline or create an overall geometric pattern on the fronts and back.*

Step 1. To alter a pattern for color-blocking, draw the desired color-block area on the commercial tissue pattern and cut on those lines as shown in Fig. 1.

Step 2. Use pattern-tracing cloth and a clear acrylic quilter's ruler to add a ⅝" seam allowance to each cut line. Cut the adjusted pieces from fabric.

Step 3. Sew the pieces of each blocked jacket section together. Tape the pattern back together along the cut lines. Compare the blocked piece to the original pattern to check the size. Trim to correct size if necessary.

Fig. 1
Draw color-block area on tissue pattern and cut as shown.

Step 4. Follow the pattern guide sheet and refer to "Reversible Single-Layer Sewing" on page 31 to sew the jacket.

Step 5. Finish seams with a mock flat-felled technique and trim the edges with the rotary cutter and a decorative blade.

Step 6. Stitch pockets in place. Use permanent fabric adhesive instead of stitching if stitch lines are undesirable on the reverse side. ✂

Reversible Garden Apron

By Marian Shenk

*The very purpose of an apron makes it the perfect candidate
for reversibility—always a fresh, clean side!*

Project Specifications

Skill Level: Beginner
Apron Size: Any size

Materials

- Simplicity pattern 9684

- 1 yard green print
- 1 yard coordinating stripe
- ¼ yard coordinating check for shoulder pieces
- 1 yard darker green print for bias binding
- All-purpose threads to match fabrics
- Basic sewing supplies and tools

Instructions

Step 1. Cut and construct two aprons following pattern instructions. Make one apron from the striped fabric and the second apron from the green print. Cut shoulder pieces for the green print apron from striped fabric. Cut shoulder pieces for the striped apron from coordinating check.

Step 2. Cut a long triple pocket from the striped fabric and a single pocket from the green print. Stitch the long triple pocket near the bottom of the green print apron. Mark and stitch two vertical dividers as shown in Fig. 1. Center the single pocket near the top of the striped apron. See photo for placement.

Fig. 1
Stitch 2 vertical dividers on pocket.

Step 3. From darker green print make 2½ yards of ¾"-wide bias as shown on page 17. Wrong sides facing, fold lengthwise, raw edges aligned; press. Place bias on ironing surface and refold, bringing long edges to center fold, wrong sides facing; press.

Step 4. Pin a strip of bias prepared in Step 3 along outer curved-and-stitched edge of long pocket. Topstitch close to each edge of bias strip.

Step 5. From one selected stripe of striped fabric cut two pieces 2½" x 14". Place on green print apron in V shape, referring to photo for placement. Stitch miter

seam at V and trim excess fabric.

Step 6. With bias prepared in Step 3, place over raw edges of V and topstitch close to each edge.

Step 7. Sandwich shoulder pieces along outside top edge of two apron fronts, right sides facing. Sew seam across top. Turn right side out and press. Repeat to attach shoulder pieces to two apron backs.

Step 8. Place two aprons together, wrong sides facing. Baste around outside edges.

Step 9. From darker green print make 5 yards of 2"-wide bias as shown on page 17. Cut four strips 1½" x 12½" for side ties.

Step 10. Wrong sides facing, fold each tie lengthwise; press. Bring long raw edges to center fold, wrong sides facing; press. Fold in half again lengthwise; press. Topstitch near folded edges.

Step 11. Position ties 13" up from bottom of apron front and back. Pin to green print side of apron, raw edges aligned.

Step 12. Bind all raw apron edges with 2"-wide bias binding, stitching ties in place with binding. ✂

Special Thanks

We would like to thank the talented sewing designers whose work is featured in this collection.

Fabrics & Supplies

Page 76: Gold Tapestry Mantel Scarf—Covington Industries Inc. Royal Brocade fabric and Wright's trim.

Page 84: Summer Fun Chair Covers—Covington Industries Inc. Portofino Collection fabric.

Page 87: Jungle Fever Shelf Cover—Fabri-Quilt Neon Forest Collection fabric.

Page 90: A Top for Every Jacket—Logantex Silk Mate fabric.

Page 108: Casserole Cozy—Wright's trim.

Page 114: Lace-Up Window Treatment—Dritz grommets and Cyrus Clark fabrics: Flirt #0176, Fancy #0175 and Flim-Flam.

Page 116: Button-Up Window Panels—JHB International buttons and Waverly fabrics: Toile #666950 and Tavern Ticking #666981.

Page 118: Prairie Points Vest—McCall's pattern 2260 and Fabri-Quilt Samba fabric by JHK Studio.

Page 126: Peekaboo Vest & Hat—Kwik Sew pattern 2459, Glick Textiles fleece fabric, Dritz Wonder Tape (double-sided basting tape) and June Tailor Heart and Star Templates.

Page 137: Pillow Panels Trio— Wright's trim and Waverly fabrics: Donnegal Rose, Wexford Plaid, Mave Check, Shannon, Celtic Quilt, Celtic Clover.

Page 145: Floral Plaid Ensemble—Waverly fabrics:

Plaid #66626 and Summer Days Floral.

Page 156: Foundation-Pieced Table Runner—Fabri-Quilt fabrics: Eastern Treasures and Patriotic assorted.

Page 158: Changeable Flap Handbag—Dan River fabric and Snap Source snaps and tools.

Page 160: Tapestry Safari Vest—Simplicity pattern 9279, Regal Fabrics Tropical Paradise Collection fabric and Beacon Fabri-Tac adhesive.

Page 162: Double-Layer Suede Vest—Simplicity pattern 9279, Toray Ultra-Suede™ (America) Inc. UltraSuede™ Light fabric, Delta Brush-On Fabric Colors paint and Fiskars rotary cutter, mat and clear ruler.

Page 164: Frayed Edges Vest—McCall's pattern 2260 and Fabric Café Chenille By The Inch.

Page 166: Suede Shirt Jacket—McCall's pattern 3401, Toray UltraSuede™ (America) Inc. UltraSuede™ Soft fabric and Fiskars rotary cutter, mat and clear ruler.

Page 168: Fleece Patch Pocket Jacket—Kwik Sew pattern 2622 and Dritz Wonder Tape (basting tape).

Page 170: Outline-Stitched Jacket—McCall's pattern 3024 and David Textiles Nordic Fleece fabric.

Page 172: Color-Block Melton Jacket—Simplicity pattern 9881 and Fiskars rotary cutter, mat and clear ruler.

Photo location courtesy of Swiss Village Retirement Center, Berne, Ind.